PORTUGU
STUDIE

VOLUME 40 NUMBER 2
2024

Guest Editor
MARIA DO CARMO PIÇARRA

Founding Editor
HELDER MACEDO

Editors
JANE-MARIE COLLINS
CATARINA FOUTO
CARLOS GARRIDO
TORI HOLMES
HILARY OWEN
EMANUELLE SANTOS
MARIA TAVARES
CLAIRE WILLIAMS

Editorial Assistant
RICHARD CORRELL

Production Editor
GRAHAM NELSON

MODERN HUMANITIES RESEARCH ASSOCIATION

PORTUGUESE STUDIES

A peer-reviewed biannual multi-disciplinary journal devoted to research on the cultures, literatures, history and societies of the Lusophone world

The **Modern Humanities Research Association** was founded in Cambridge in 1918 and has become an international organization with members in all parts of the world. It is a registered charity number 1064670, and a company limited by guarantee, registered in England number 3446016. Its main object is to encourage advanced study and research in modern and medieval European languages, literatures, and cultures by its publication of journals, book series, and its Style Guide. Further information about the activities of the Association and individual membership may be obtained from the Membership Secretary, email membership@mhra.org.uk, or from the website at: **www.mhra.org.uk**

ISSN 0267–5315 (print) ISSN 2222–4270 (online)
ISBN 978-1-83954-285-5

PORTUGUESE STUDIES VOL. 40 NO. 2

FILMED REPRESENTATIONS OF FORMER PORTUGUESE ASIA AND THE INDIAN OCEAN

CONTENTS

NOTES FOR CONTRIBUTORS

Articles to be considered for publication may be on any subject within the field but must not exceed 7,500 words, and should be submitted in a form ready for publication in English, sent as an email attachment to the Editorial Assistant at portuguese@mhra.org.uk.

Contributions whose standard of English is inadequate will be returned. Any quotations in Portuguese must be accompanied by an English translation. Submissions in Portuguese may be considered, but full peer review and publication will be conditional on provision of a satisfactory translation by or on behalf of the author. The Editorial Assistant may undertake translations on request for a reasonable charge.

Text and references should conform precisely to the conventions of the *MHRA Style Guide*, 3rd edn, 2013 (978-1-78188-009-8), £9.50, $19.00, €12.00, obtainable in print or online version from www.style.mhra.org.uk. All articles are subject to independent, anonymous peer review by experts in the field; authors receive written feedback on the editors' decision and guidance on any revisions required. *Portuguese Studies* regrets it must charge contributors for the cost of corrections in proof deemed excessive.

It is a condition of publication in this journal that authors of articles and reviews assign copyright, including electronic copyright, to the MHRA. Inter alia, this allows the General Editor to deal efficiently and consistently with requests from third parties for permission to reproduce material. The journal has been published simultaneously in printed and electronic form since January 2001. Permission, without fee, for authors to use their own material in other publications, after a reasonable period of time has elapsed, is not normally withheld. Authors may make closed-access deposit of accepted manuscripts in their academic institution's digital repository upon acceptance. Full open access to the accepted manuscript is permitted no sooner than 12 months following publication of the Contribution by the MHRA. Contributions may also be republished on authors' personal websites without seeking further permission from the Association, but no earlier than 12 months after publication by the MHRA.

Portuguese Studies aims to publish reviews of recent books within its field of interest in each issue. Publishers wishing to put forward a book for review should contact one or both of the Reviews Editors, Maria Tavares (m.tavares@qub.ac.uk) and Carlos Garrido (carlos.garridocastellano@ucc.ie).

Introduction

Maria do Carmo Piçarra

The Portuguese Estado Novo dictatorship (1933–74) made recurrent use of film propaganda to assert its colonial power. Use of this resource increased from 1951, to affirm Portuguese multiracialism in the face of international pressure directed at the regime for its persistence in retaining its colonies. When the Brazilian sociologist Gilberto Freyre coined the concept of Luso-tropicalism, the Estado Novo was only too happy to adopt it in support of its official rhetoric. It is of significance that only after this date did the dictatorship finally set about filming 'Portuguese Asia' and increasing its control over independent local film production.

In Portugal, a want is still felt of research studies about how the films directed by Portuguese filmmakers during the Estado Novo represented the colonies and recorded the political and ideological changes that shaped life under colonialism.[1] Furthermore, these filmic representations of colonialism, propagandistic in their essence, have remained largely unquestioned, to the extent that, in the discourse involving colonial cinema, the term 'empire' is still commonly conflated with 'African empire'.

The last territories of the 'Portuguese Orient', Macau, Goa, Daman and Diu, and Timor, have limited access to colonial footage, which has been kept mainly in Portugal. There is no official colonial filmography, and no information has been categorized with regards to what institutions may have collected films or possessed documentation. The difficulty in gaining access to films and the lack of organized information about colonial filmography limits knowledge of this field and, consequently, of life under colonialism, hindering the debate about how the colonial period may be imagined, and post-independence life projected, by these very same communities.

'Portuguese Orient' was the expression employed by the regime to name an 'imagined community' to the East, corresponding to a territory which had endured a Portuguese presence from the beginning of the sixteenth century until the first few decades of the eighteenth. Notwithstanding a fading Portuguese presence in the region that would eventually become residual and the fact that, in Portugal, the previous regimes had progressively shifted any

---

[1] With the exception of Paulo Cunha and myself, the authors of the articles published here were not part of the team behind the project 'CINEASIA — Film Representations of "Portuguese Asia"', which I supervised between February 2022 and March 2023, with the support of ICNOVA-FSCH. However, this edition of *Portuguese Studies* meets the aim set out in the CINEASIA project: to contribute to an account of the impact that the filmic representations of 'Portuguese Asia' imposed by the Estado Novo had on the socio-cultural memories and identity narratives that persist.

Portuguese Studies vol. 40 no. 2 (2024), doi:10.1353/port.00010, pp. 115–20
© Modern Humanities Research Association 2024

imaginary grandeur linked to the East first to Brazil, and then, during the dictatorship, to the African colonies, this expression was still employed for political purposes, and was quite common in propaganda films. This insistence on such an expression bears several implications, the most important being self-reference, that is, the primacy given to the idea of being Portuguese. Another, which derives from the first, is that it designates the diverse territories that fall under Portuguese colonial rule.

Its use was combined advantageously (from the Estado Novo's viewpoint) with the concept of Luso-tropicalism coined by Brazilian sociologist Gilberto Freyre, which also propagated a series of basic and simplistic assumptions about the colonies, based upon a racial theory rooted in the mixed-race lineage of the Portuguese, and a supposed multiculturalism resting on the capability the average Lusitanian, and Portuguese culture in general, possessed to adapt to tropical settings.

Freyre's concept, which he first enunciated in Goa at the start of a long trip to the Portuguese 'overseas provinces' (as they were then known), shares common attributes with the ideas identified by Edward Said as being intrinsic to the notion of Orientalism. Defined by Edward Said as a western style of speech developed to justify control over the Orient, Orientalism was anchored in anthropological, biological, linguistic, racial, and historical theses about humanity, and certain economic and sociological development theories addressing cultural and religious aspects, to frame knowledge and legitimize western ascendancy. These 'scientific' theses at the service of colonial projects legitimized a western voice that spoke in the name of eastern territories and helped impose a material servility towards the West. Making use of an artificial ontological and epistemological distinction between regions of the world, European imperialism thus justified the implementation of the social hierarchies it subsequently sustained through colonial violence. This process asserted the pacifism of Christian civilization, while also empowering it as vital in the 'necessary' process of 'evolutionary' promotion of oriental folks, who happened to live in the 'infancy of humanity', or the regeneration of local customs belonging to civilizations which had become 'decadent' or immoral.[2] The idea of a supposed mission to civilize peoples whose cultural, moral, and social codes failed to coincide with a European-Christian compass is central to Orientalism, since it served a colonial power structure short of the raw materials and labour-power necessary to sustain an Industrial Revolution then at full steam.

When Freyre looked to the Orient, he did so from the viewpoint of the Iberian West, Christian and patriarchal. Already in works such as *Casa-Grande & Senzala* (1933), he proposes that it was from Portugal that a positive colonialism developed, based on a range of 'good practices' anchored in a

---

[2]   In this sentence, all the inverted commas are mine, indicating words and expressions that were once used in a colonial situation and which I therefore point out as problematic.

mission that was evangelizing, but also — paradoxically — ecumenical. This 'positive' colonialism was put under strain, in the nineteenth century, by the bourgeois-industrial West. The Portuguese empire was, according to Freyre, multiracial and, for that reason, ultimately integrating, in contrast with the 'other' West which Portugal had no part in, overbearing and obsessed with profit — a vision hardly reconcilable with the history of Portuguese maritime expansion.

When Freyre visited 'Portuguese India', he arrived already armed with a series of tropes about the distinctive features of the 'Portuguese Orient', capable of creating, according to him, an altogether different 'Orientalism'. It should be noted that Freyre never set foot in Macau, let alone 'Portuguese Timor', but still made assumptions that then served — and still do — the official discourse about these territories. Freyre's views, based as they were on oversimplifications, and smoothed out to the point where they could serve the regime's propaganda, bore implications for the situations under analysis, despite the specificities that separated them. If, in the rhetoric of propaganda films, the recurrent axiom is that each of these oriental territories is more Portuguese than the next, there are still, with regards to religious ecumenism, marked discursive differences between Macau and India, on the one hand, and Timor, on the other, where the latter is often contrasted with the former two for the docility of its population. As for Macau, energy goes into trying to quell its widespread image as a 'gambling inferno', rife with opium consumption, prostitution, arms trafficking, and corruption, portraying it, instead, as a peaceful city, locked in the middle of a troubled part of the Orient, but open to all religions. The focus on religious freedom in 'Portuguese India' includes references to the Catholicism of the population, attested mostly through the presentation of religious landmarks — predominantly ruins — from the most relevant period of Portuguese occupation, and images of Hindu temples.

This collection intends to contribute to characterizing the impact of cinematographic representations of 'Portuguese Asia' propelled by the dictatorship in socio-cultural memories and narrative identities, critically exhuming filmic archives and analysing contemporary film production. Underlying this aim is the idea that the diverse ways in which Portuguese citizens or those of former 'Portuguese Asia' conceive their own identity and that of other members of the *Comunidade dos Países de Língua Portuguesa* (CPLP) is traceable in the archives. Contemporary cinematographic representations of the Eastern territories by Portuguese directors or by local directors often directly address identity issues and the persistent memories of the 'imagined community', which they criticize, complicating the narrative of the previous official discourse that somehow persists because no explicit official counter-narrative has emerged, and sometimes, in a more subtle or even unconscious way, they propose different representations, as could only be expected given the complexity of reality and the historical, social and political changes that have taken place in the meantime. Either way, however, they generally start from the recognition that there has been a sedimentation of representations that need to be questioned and a lack of representation of certain cultural minorities.

*   *   *   *   *

The first article in this volume, 'Palimpsestic Orientalism: Deciphering the Layered Reconstructions of the Portuguese-Macau Film Co-production *The Bewitching Braid* (1996)', by **Yuxuan Liu**, examines the epistemological underpinnings of Orientalism, as embedded in the collective psyche of the Macanese community, through the lens of Senna Fernandes's celebrated novel *A Trança Feiticeira* [The Bewitching Braid] and the 1996 film adaptation of the same name, directed by Yuanyuan Cai. Focusing on the intersection of colonial narratives and Orientalist thought, it uncovers the psychological divide that has long rationalized systemic exploitation and dominance over the Other, through a blend of literary criticism and film analysis. Yuxuan Liu proposes that the novel and its cinematic representation, which delve deep into native Macanese identity across historical epochs, have not been examined from an Orientalist perspective. Her study intends to fill this gap by dissecting the layers of Orientalism and narrative development in Fernandes's work, offering new insights into the construction of Macanese identity and associated cultural narratives. It discusses in detail how the profound social fissures, racial complexities, and power imbalances concealed within the film's layers are uncovered, and how the timeless themes of identity, cultural integration, and social tensions have permeated Macau's history and Sino-Portuguese relations and shaped the region.

Maria do Carmo Piçarra's article, '"Portuguese India": Between the Desire for a Konkani Cinema and the Paradoxes of Filmed Propaganda', focuses on how, notwithstanding a vibrant film exhibition culture, Konkani cinema never gained traction, but nevertheless there appeared, during the Estado Novo, a simultaneous stream of propaganda films that aimed to project the image of a supposed Luso-tropical idyll, favouring religious themes, and extoling multiculturalism and miscegenation — concomitantly contradicted by the tensions manifest in films with a political-military focus. Piçarra proposes that the lack of Portuguese films resulted not just from a physical distance from the metropolis and the costs of production: despite the regime's tardiness in appointing the filming of these territories, the symbolic value of that 'imagined community' was better disseminated by a kind of cinematic omission. When production did take place, it ignored certain aspects of reality as much as it filmed others, framing them inside a vague Luso-oriental rhetoric which concealed anything that contradicted the prevalent 'order of discourse'.

'A Transcivilizational Island: Paulo Rocha's *A Ilha dos Amores*' is a reflection on the mediating role of cinema in evoking and reframing the past. In it, **Paulo Cunha** analyses how *A Ilha dos Amores* (1982) illustrates the relationship between West and East based on the life of Portuguese poet and diplomat Wenceslau de Moraes, who lived in Macau (1891–98) and in Japan (1898–1929), where he died. Cunha presents his reflections on how the film is also marked by the work of the Chinese poet Chu Yuan (343 BC–278 BC) and the Portuguese poet Luís Vaz de Camões (1524–1580), in an intersection of literary and cultural universes that makes *A Ilha dos Amores* a transcivilizational narrative.

In her article '*Entre eu e Deus* by Yara Costa: An Unprecedented Representation of the Island of Mozambique', **Jessica Falconi** analyses how in *Entre eu e Deus* [Between God and I] (2018), filmed on the Island of Mozambique, the Mozambican director Yara Costa produces an original representation of a crucial place in the Mozambican cultural imagination. She proposes that the documentary's primary objective is to challenge images, representations and crystallized perceptions about the Island of Mozambique, Mozambican cultural identity and Islamic fundamentalism.

In 'East Timor in Margarida Gil's *Bitter Flowers*: The Power of the Unrooted Underdog', **Ana Isabel Soares** starts out from a detailed analysis of *Flores Amargas* [Bitter Flowers] (1989), by the Portuguese director Margarida Gil, to appreciate the multiplicity of European perspectives on East Timor. The quasi-fictional feature is set in an East Timorese community of political refugees on the outskirts of Lisbon during the Indonesian occupation of Timor. The Timorese are characterized as a homogeneous and relatively tight-knit group who revive the habits and traditions of the geographically distant homeland but seem to accept the welcoming linguistic environment it shares with the post-colonial metropolis. Among readings of paternalism, a zeal for cultural heritage, and layers of domination, the film establishes a primarily human geography, based on looks and facial expressions, in which the work of light and shade plays a fundamental role. Nine years later, East Timor is revisited in Gil's *Anjo da Guarda* [Guardian Angel] (1998), in which the Asian territory serves as a backdrop for the memories of a recently deceased father and for the Freudian tribulations of a psychiatrist in a mid-life crisis. Soares suggests an allegorical reading of the end of the colonizing homeland and the difficulty in affirming the new Portugal, grappling with the emotional relationship with a past whose memory does not fade.

In '*Adventures in Mozambique and the Portuguese Tendency to Forget*: A Radical Critique of Portuguese Late Colonialism by Ângela Ferreira', **Lurdes Macedo** and **Viviane Almeida** present a critical reflection on how this film contrasts two realities experienced in Mozambique during the late colonial period — that of the Portuguese settlers and that of the indigenous Maconde — through an artistic composition starting from a reinterpretation of four archives. The authors propose that Ferreira's film is a radical critique of the Portuguese colonial system in this territory between the 1950s and 1970s, based on the application of the concept of 'the return of the gaze' renewed by Ferreira to her methodology of constructing the filmic object. In their conclusions,

Macedo and Almeida point out that by applying her own concept to make this film, Ferreira proposes three possibilities: the creative, which is related with 'the return of the gaze' of the camera; the relational, connected with 'the return of the gaze' of the spectator; and the communicative, that finally allows the artist to say what she wants to say about the late colonialism in Mozambique.

Finally, **R. Benedito Ferrão** interviews **Bardroy Barretto**, director of the Konkani-language film *Nachom-ia Kumpasar* (2015), set in Goa and Bombay of the 1960s. The film tells the story of the contribution made by Goan musicians to Indian cinema through the lives of characters who are inspired by real-life entertainers Lorna Cordeiro and Chris Perry. Even as the film demonstrates how Goan music with its Portuguese influences created the soundtrack for Bollywood in the second half of the twentieth century, *Nachom-ia Kumpasar* also bears witness to the part played by the Indian film industry and film history in undermining the legacy of Goan musicians. 'How Bollywood Lost its Goan Rhythm' clarifies the perspective of Bardroy Barretto on contemporary Goan cinema while Ferrão's analysis enquires into the importance of Goan music-making in the creation of the twentieth-century Bollywood soundtrack. Ferrão argues that the mark Goans left on Indian cinema's soundscape not only harks back to Goa's Portuguese past but also raises a discordant note about India's culturally consumptive relationship with the region.

Palimpsestic Orientalism: Deciphering the Layered Reconstructions of the Portuguese-Macau Film Co-production *The Bewitching Braid* (1996)

Yuxuan Liu

University of Massachusetts–Dartmouth

Introduction

In *The Bewitching Braid*, a mesmerizing portrait of 1930s Macau, a narrative vortex comes to life: Adozindo, a young Portuguese aristocrat, and A-Leng, a Chinese water carrier, are caught up in a romance that is both transcendent and entangled in a web of historical and cultural tension. In the film's opening tableau, Henrique de Senna Fernandes, the author of the original Portuguese novel, is elegantly attired in a suit and contemplatively smoking a pipe. Addressing the audience with solemn introspection, he proclaims, 'This is not an ordinary braid; this is a fascinating braid. Should you entangle yourself within its coils, extrication is a formidable challenge, as I am intimately aware.'[1] Senna Fernandes bridges the gap between the written word and its cinematic interpretation, inviting the audience to go beyond the surface narrative and explore its more profound, labyrinthine, personal and emotional depths. As the luminous title of the movie graces the darkened theatre, it entices and unsettles in equal measure. The braid, also called a queue or cue, represents more than a hairstyle for Western audiences shaped by centuries of Eastern artistic, literary, and filmic imagery; it also epitomizes the mystique of the Orient, with the cultural disdain and pejorative stereotyping it entails. Braids were a significant visual element of the 'yellow peril' image that pervaded twentieth-century European and American cinema; they framed the cunning, malevolent, and sinister face of Fu Manchu (the famous villain created by British author Sax Rohmer) and the bare foreheads of the Manchurian officials of the Qing dynasty, those personifiers of feudal oppression, ignorance, and the Orient's peculiarly feminine, introverted, and amiable temperament.[2] Senna Fernandes's

---

[1] *The Bewitching Braid*, dir. by Yuanyuan Cai (Zhujiang Film Studio Company, the Cai Brothers (Macau) Film Co. Ltd, the China Film Co-Production Corporation, 1996), 00:00:13–00:00:39. All translations from Portuguese and Chinese are my own unless otherwise noted.
[2] Jason Crum, '"Out of the Glamorous, Mystic East": Techno-Orientalism in Early Twentieth-Century U.S. Radio Broadcasting', in *Techno-Orientalism: Imagining Asia in Speculative Fiction,*

Portuguese Studies vol. 40 no. 2 (2024), doi:10.1353/port.00011, pp. 121–41
© Modern Humanities Research Association 2024

commentary creates a dissonance that subverts the collective imagination, drowning the viewer in a sea of conflicting emotions and narratives, prompting them to question how a symbol of cultural ridicule synonymous with ignorance and backwardness can metamorphose into a seductive motif. It also reinforces the film's thematic fabric and alludes to the intricate unfolding narrative of cultural identity.

The present study examines the epistemological underpinnings of Orientalism, as embedded in the collective psyche of the Macanese community, through the lens of Senna Fernandes's celebrated 1993 novel *A trança feiticeira* [*The Bewitching Braid*] and the 1996 film adaptation of the same name, directed by Yuanyuan Cai.[3] It focuses on the intersection of colonial narratives and Orientalist thought, uncovering the psychological divide that has long rationalized systemic exploitation and dominance over the Other through a blend of literary criticism and film analysis. The novel and its cinematic representation, which delve deep into native Macanese identity across historical epochs, have not previously been examined from an Orientalist perspective. The present study fills this gap by dissecting the intricate layers of Orientalism and narrative development in Fernandes's work, offering new insights into the construction of Macanese identity and associated cultural narratives. The profound social fissures, racial complexities, and power imbalances concealed within the film's layers are uncovered, and the timeless themes of identity, cultural integration, and social tensions that have permeated Macau's history and Sino-Portuguese relations and shaped the region are discussed in detail.

Evolving Orientalism in Macanese Cinema

Edward Said's *Orientalism* reveals the dynamic process by which the West came to dominate the Orient, e.g. through meticulously constructed imaginative geographies and narratives. It also serves as a compass for navigating the Macanese identity.[4] For more than four centuries, Macau's status as a free port with a Southern European flair and Latin cultural overtones that survive on the edge of the Chinese mainland has made the place a vibrant contact zone for different cultures, races, and societies, and a historical container of ancient East–West power dynamics. A group known as the *filhos da terra* [children of the land] evolved during four hundred and twenty years of Portuguese rule, emerging from the integration of Portuguese immigrants and various ethnic groups from China, Japan, India, and Southeast Asia. More than a demographic phenomenon, these individuals are now woven into the fabric of Macau, holding key professional and social roles, particularly in cultural

History, and Media, ed. by David S. Roh, Betsy Huang and Greta A. Niu (New Brunswick, NJ: Rutgers University Press, 2015), pp. 40–51 (p. 42).
3   Henrique de Senna Fernandes, *The Bewitching Braid*, trans. by David Brookshaw (Hong Kong: Hong Kong University Press, 2004).
4   Edward W. Said, *Orientalism*, 1st Vintage Books edn (New York: Vintage Books, 1979), pp. 55–57.

dissemination, printing, and education.[5] Senna Fernandes, a distinguished member of the Macanese community — and of the sixth generation of a respected family whose lineage extends over more than 270 years — exemplifies this deep socio-cultural connection. His paternal great-grandmother, Countess Ana Teresa Vieira Ribeiro, his mother, Maria Luísa de Oliveira Rodrigues, and his wife, Maria Teresa Hó, were all of Chinese descent, which afforded him a range of linguistic skills and a profound cultural acumen, granting him insights into the collective psyche of Macau's diverse community. His ability to negotiate between estrangement and proximity and to understand both self and society allowed him to capture the essence of a society in transition. In its transition from a ruling class in the colonial era to a merely privileged one thereafter, the native Macanese community, as insiders and outsiders bearing an Eastern and Western lineage, has profoundly influenced artistic and cultural expressions of the region's identity. Said's emphasis on the deep roots of Orientalism and the hegemonic structure of colonial and imperial histories is particularly relevant in this context — as is Foucault's concept of discursive power (a central tenet of *Orientalism*).[6] Both perspectives make it possible to scrutinize the present film as a vital cultural product, focusing on the power dynamics embedded in its forms of representation — e.g. the right to narrate and who is being narrated.

In examining the underpinnings of Orientalism within Macanese cinema, it is instructive to trace its evolution from the earliest films, such as *Caminhos Longos* [*Long Way*], where the storylines were based on local culture, to *The Bewitching Braid*. *Long Way* (1955), which aligned with Portuguese cultural paradigms, was the first wholly Macanese-produced film. Meanwhile, *The Bewitching Braid* presents the perspective of the native Macanese *filhos da terra*, unravelling a complex fusion of cultural identities. Although there is no shortage of plots relating to or set in Macau in mainstream global cinematic narratives, both of the films in question mark pivotal moments in Macau's twentieth-century cultural history, a period when local narratives and aesthetics began to be taken seriously. *Long Way* was produced by the Eurasia Film Company, a Sino-Portuguese venture. It stood at the intersection between the art of colonial and Luso-tropicalist cinema and the political agenda of the Estado Novo.[7] However, the original version was lost, and only secondary sources and peripheral literature remained. The absence of detailed documentation and related scholarly work, along with a lack of economic and institutional support for the region's industry led to a public misunderstanding or oversimplification of Macau's early film history.[8]

---

[5]   Chi Chiu Fok, *From Monotheism to Polytheism: A Research on the Changing Macanese Religious Belief* (Beijing: Social Sciences Academic Press, 2009), pp. 2, 53.

[6]   Said, *Orientalism*, p. 23.

[7]   Ana Catarina Almeida Leite, 'Cleansing Macau's Image as the "Wickedest City in the World": Eurasia, Long Way, and Luso-Tropical Film Production in Macau in the 1950s', *Modern Asian Studies*, 55.6 (2021), 1795–1847 (p. 1798).

[8]   João Botas, '"Caminhos Longos", 1955', *Macau Antigo*, 3 May 2009 <https://macauantigo.blogspot.com/ 2009/05/caminhos-longos-1955.html> [accessed 22 August 2024].

Long Way's self-authorization and internalization of Orientalist themes of conversion, reformation, and rejuvenation revealed that the exotic Other could be transformed, civilized, and made to conform to the colonial ideal. The film's denouement, wherein an Eastern smuggler finds redemption through a Western police officer, symbolically portrays the West as a corrective to the East's perceived moral flaws, underscoring the ethos of a self-styled saviour to idealize, assimilate, and domesticate the Other under a guise of benevolent superiority. *Long Way*'s depiction of interracial relationships is based on gendered racial hierarchies. The exploration of love, which is conducted primarily through two contrasting love triangles involving Portuguese, mixed-race, and Chinese characters, offers a tangible representation of the cultural and racial intermingling that characterizes Macau's history. The director uses Mestizo female characters and those of Oriental origin as symbols of exoticism, blending strangeness with familiarity. Such a duality reflects the colonial desire both to embrace and control the Oriental Other, reinforcing stereotypical contrasts between Western masculinity and Eastern femininity, highlighting the dissonance between external colonial narratives and the internal realities of Macau. This representation, however, is superfluous to Macau's inherent Oriental ethos. Ultimately, the film's fantastical colonial vision masks the underlying socio-economic and racial complexities of the region.[9]

Contrastingly, the latter Macanese film, *The Bewitching Braid*, stands out as an emblematic case study in the broader sphere of film adaptation. In bringing together Adozindo (a Portuguese man) and A-Leng (a Chinese woman), the director transcends homogeneous Orientalist frameworks and monolithic Eurocentric representations of cultural identity, marking a paradigmatic shift away from a rigid and essentialist perspective. As has been noted, *The Bewitching Braid* draws its narrative depth and cultural authenticity significantly from the position of Senna Fernandes, who was able to capture the diverse experiences of the Macanese, weaving them into a rich and ever-evolving East–West interplay. The author's position as an inheritor of the legacy of Portuguese colonialism and its romanticized view of the Orient enables him to conjure narratives that both challenge and perpetuate traditional perspectives. However, the film's representation of the *filhos da terra* is far from neutral.[10] Rooted in the East yet gravitating towards European heritage, this community predominantly identifies with Portuguese culture, and this influenced Fernandes's narrative and the film adaptation of his book. This disconnect calls to mind Said's *Culture and Imperialism*, where colonial history jars with corresponding literary and cultural narratives that are often neglected in academic discourse.[11] The present study endeavours to fill this lacuna. The analysis adopts a comparative

---

[9]   Ana Catarina Almeida Leite, 'Cleansing Macau's Image', p. 1822.
[10]   Chang Seng Li, *The Formation, Development and Changes of the Native Communities in Macau during the Ming and Qing Dynasties* (Beijing: Zhonghua Book Company, 2007), p. 3.
[11]   Edward W. Said, *Culture and Imperialism*, 1st Vintage Books edn (New York: Vintage Books, 1994), p. 43.

methodology, filtering Fernandes's textual narrative through its hypertextual cinematic representation and unveiling the underlying disequilibrium of power, covert reductionist pejorative tendencies, and overt societal segregation in both media. The study concludes that the original text and the Cai brothers' cinematic interpretation were pivotal in redefining and reshaping the discourse of Orientalism within the unique context of Macau's cultural and political landscape.

Historical Parallels, Nostalgia, and Identity in Senna Fernandes's Macau

Senna Fernandes's storytelling traverses themes of love, folklore, and the humanistic environment of Macau, highlighting a nostalgia for pre-modern times and juxtaposing them with the challenges posed by issues of identity and cultural disorientation during the transfer of sovereignty. The author, who was born in 1923, attempts to resurrect the golden 1930s, an era of modernization and urbanization for Macau. This timeframe, marked by significant historical events such as the Second World War, the Sino-Japanese War, and the Pacific Wars, was also characterized by dramatic economic fluctuations, including a boom and the subsequent collapse of the Hong Kong stock market.[12] Senna Fernandes captures the complexities and contradictions of this tumultuous period, focusing on the intertwined fates and distinct experiences of the native Macanese and Chinese communities. The 1930s also saw advances in communication, construction, and transportation, bridging the gap between East and West; cultural commodities like the Portuguese film *Canção de Lisboa* [*The Song of Lisbon*] (1933), theatre, the folk tradition *Serração da Velha*,[13] and Latin American music played a crucial role in this integration.[14] The impermanence of geopolitical entities, the outbreak of war, the shifting fortunes of nations, and the fluidity of identity in times of crisis inevitably affect individual destinies and psyches, especially those of the *filhos da terra*. One of the most important features of inter-cultural engagement in this period was the increase in interracial relationships and miscegenation, leading as it did to the integration of different worldviews, traditions, and values.[15]

The Bewitching Braid and another of Fernandes's works, *Amor e dedinhos de pé* [*Love and Tiny Toes*] (1986), also made into a film, are consistent in their storyline and thematic structure. They both offer insights into the life of the upper-middle-class Macanese community during times of historical transition. The respective protagonists, Francisco Frontaria and Adozindo — aristocrats exiled in the Chinese community due to romantic entanglements — find

---

[12] Senna Fernandes, *The Bewitching Braid*, pp. 182–83.
[13] The *Serração da Velha*, introduced by Portuguese settlers, is adapted in Macau as a symbolic masquerade marking seasonal renewal, typically held during Carnival and Lent.
[14] Henrique de Senna Fernandes, 'Cinema Em Macau III (1932–36)', *Revista de Cultura*, 23.2 (1995), 151–52.
[15] Chi Chiu Fok, *From Monotheism to Polytheism*, p. 45.

redemption through female characters, thus mirroring Fernandes's experience. Senna Fernandes, whose family falls into bankruptcy, develops a crush on a Chinese girl with a braid in the alleys of Macau and eventually marries a Chinese woman. The character's retrospection, which lends the narrative an emotional depth and historical authenticity, is rooted in the author's engagement with East and West. Fernandes's dialectical self-exploration highlights enduring struggles with themes of identity, colonization, and interracial relations. However, in the context of the history of post-colonial studies, his reminiscences appear to stem from an innate urge to reassert a fragmented identity, which is particularly important for communities undergoing socio-cultural metamorphosis. Senna Fernandes's insightful allusions to significant transformations in the urban landscape of Macau — including the abandonment of traditional braids by Chinese women in favour of short, modern hairstyles and the bulldozing and remodelling of gardens, flowerbeds, and fountains in Portuguese neighbourhoods — reveal a broader theme: a pervasive nostalgia for pre-modern Macau.[16]

A comparative analysis of these novels unravels the thematic parallels, continuities, and divergences of Senna Fernandes's literary canon and makes possible an exegesis of their underlying thematic strata. Both books offer insights into the socio-cultural zeitgeist at the historical junctures of the nineteenth and twentieth centuries. *Love and Tiny Toes* is set against the backdrop of the 1887 Sino-Portuguese Treaty of Peking, which made Macau an official Portuguese colony, initiating a succession of geopolitical changes in the ensuing century. Notably, Senna Fernandes's presence as a special guest of the Beijing government at the 1987 signing of the Joint Declaration on the Question of Macau was a sign of his intimate connection with these transformative historical moments. This close encounter with an essential and transformative chapter in the history of Macau's development and direct witness to the conclusion of the Sino-Portuguese treaty of 1887 left the writer deeply shaken. *Love and Tiny Toes* speaks of the Chinese populace's calls for its abolition, while *The Bewitching Braid* marks the treaty's end. In the 1920s, during the nationalist awakening under Sun Yat-sen, the Beiyang and Kuomintang governments, despite their intentions to revisit the treaty, refrained from making explicit claims to sovereignty over Macau due to geopolitical pressures. The 1928 Sino-Portuguese Treaty of Friendship and Trade, comprising only five articles and omitting any mention of Macau, reaffirmed Portuguese governance of Macau in accordance with the original treaty. Macau was left in geopolitical purgatory, with its fate again in the balance and subject to passive speculation.[17] The narrative of *The Bewitching Braid* masterfully intertwines Portuguese colonial anxieties and the

---

[16] Senna Fernandes, *The Bewitching Braid*, pp. 188–95.
[17] Zhong Peng Zhang, 'Organization and Party Activities of the Macao Branch of the Kuomintang (1919–1949)', ed. by Cultural Affairs Bureau of Government of Macao SAR, *Revista de Cultura* (2011), 67–82 (p. 67).

awakening of Chinese nationalism.[18] Senna Fernandes's decision to publish his novels during Macau's critical transition to Beijing in the 1990s speaks volumes about his deep engagement with the cultural disorientation and identity crises experienced by the Macanese community. This period is a prime example of the political fervour generated by the convergence of Eastern and Western political trajectories. Senna Fernandes's narratives poignantly capture the Macanese people's nostalgia, cultural rootlessness, existential dilemmas, and disquieting pain. The author's sharp social commentary and meticulous characterizations, especially his portrayal of Macanese myopia — the price of commodities was prioritized over major socio-political events like the Sino-Japanese War and European upheavals — contrast starkly with that of his counterparts.[19] A tendency towards escapism and disengagement rendered the community passive, allowing external forces to dictate their fate without any possibility of resistance.

Cinematic Techniques and Visual Dichotomies

Gérard Genette's conceptualization of palimpsests enriches our understanding of film adaptations by providing a framework for understanding the ways a director can transform and reinterpret original literary texts. Film adaptation is a hypertextual process: the audience is led by the director's vision, wherein the traditional and singular linear storytelling is rewritten as a holistic, multisensory narrative involving camera language, scene composition, lighting, and sound design.[20] This provides an immersive and intertextual experience that allows the audience to collectively and synchronously resonate with the film's themes and narratives. The palimpsest approach to film adaptation mirrors the process of re-engraving parchment, where the traces and essence of the original narrative remain visible while being enhanced and recontextualized by new layers. Douglas Ishii uses this approach to show how Oriental narratives are treated in film adaptations: the future is superimposed onto a colonial past, enabling Orientals to assert and/or resist perspectives and discourses that were traditionally dominated by Western perspectives. Cinema is imbued with a form of empowerment, rectifying historical imbalances in representation and creating a narrative space for reinterpretation.[21] The adaptation of *The Bewitching Braid* is an example of a strategic shift in cultural representation in that it de-centres the Orientalist storyline of the original novel. The film

---

[18] Sheng Hua Lou, 'Passing Away and New Life: Changes in Macao's Folk Associations and Its Clues', in *Nova História de Macau*, ed. by Zhi Liang Wu, Guo Ping Jin, and Kai Jian Tang, 4 vols (Macau: Fundação Macau, 2008), III, 884–87.

[19] Senna Fernandes, *The Bewitching Braid*, p. 183.

[20] Gérard Genette, *Palimpsests: Literature in the Second Degree*, trans. by Channa Newman and Claude Doubinsky (Lincoln: University of Nebraska Press, 1997), p. 5.

[21] Douglas Ishii, 'Palimpsestic Orientalisms and Antiblackness; or, Joss Whedon's Grand Vision of an Asian/American Tomorrow', in *Techno-Orientalism*, ed. by Roh et al., pp. 180–92 (p. 181).

subtly addresses the divisions and confrontations between the Chinese and Portuguese communities in Macau, though not through explicit dialogue or confrontation but through nuanced visual and symbolic language.

Phase One: Spatial and Religious Dichotomies

The first phase of the storyline illustrates the dichotomy between and the interconnectedness of Macau's elegant Santo António parish and the impoverished Horta da Mitra district, capturing the contrasting realities of the central protagonists, Adozindo and A-Leng, whose lives, beliefs, and families encapsulate the essence of Macau's diverse identity. The director astutely employs semiotics and visual grammar to articulate these abstract cultural disparities, transforming them into a tangible and comprehensible visual language. The interplay of cultural symbols — daily practices, rituals, attire, and landscapes — constitutes a form of dialogue, mapping out cultural geographies that accentuate social stratification, religious beliefs, and class distinctions, and effectively delineating the cultural dichotomy between East and West. In the novel, Adozindo and A-Leng live parallel lives, only coming together through a serendipitous encounter at the Largo do Lilau well. The film juxtaposes the well (emblematic of Eastern restraint and conservatism in the context of romantic encounters) with a white pier (a metaphor for Western exploration and adventure). The director builds on the narrative trajectory by allowing the audience to accompany Adozindo and his tagalong Florêncio through the neighbourhoods of Macau, where they are introduced to a grandiose juxtaposition of a Chinese lion dance and a lavish Portuguese masquerade ball. The film's director uses this backdrop to juxtapose the figure of Tudigong,[22] deeply entrenched in Chinese folklore and Taoist tradition, with Catholic and carnival elements. The diverse celebrations of the Pre-Lenten season offer possibilities for collective transgression and subversion, e.g. the suspension of the prevailing colonial order, enabling an exploration of alternative realities and identities. As such, the director draws heavily on the traditions and spectacles of the author's aristocratic family.[23] The contrast between the opulent, silver-purple Portuguese masquerade ball and the traditional, black-red Chinese full moon banquet, and between the pristine, open aristocratic villa in Santo António and the enclosed, grey Horta da Mitra, starkly emphasizes the tension between light and darkness, openness and enclosure, and modernity and tradition. Adozindo and A-Leng's contrasting residential settings are a metaphor for the deep-seated class divisions, cultural disparities, and profound ideological schisms of Macau's inhabitants. This difference is also manifested

---

[22] Tudigong is the deity responsible for safeguarding a specific locality, closely tied to agricultural prosperity and communal welfare. In Macau, this tradition is deeply embedded in local culture, with numerous shrines and altars dedicated to Tudigong across public spaces, homes and businesses.

[23] Fernando Sales Lopes, 'O Carnaval', *Dialogando, Talking* (2006), 4–10 (p. 9).

in the protagonists' sartorial choices: Adozindo — a dashing yet dissolute aristocrat — becomes unexpectedly enthralled by the vibrant spectacle of the lion dance, especially when he discovers the lead dancer is a young woman. His white attire and trousers contrast with A-Leng's striking, raven-black braid. But their appearance, while reflecting cultural variations in romantic expression, is also used to construct a semiotic framework. The director infuses scenes with an abstract, inherently Oriental chromaticism and contrast, accentuating the remnants of Western colonial influence and the significant cultural divide between the two ethnicities. The fleeting interaction between the two characters leaves an indelible mark on Adozindo, who grapples with aristocratic ennui and the prospect of his arranged marriage with the affluent widow Lucrécia, compelling him to search the labyrinthine Chinese quarters for A-Leng. This invites the audience to explore Macau's geography and the communal differentiation it fosters.

Macau underwent tumultuous upheavals from the seventeenth century. An influx of Chinese immigrants, predominantly from the Lingnan and Fujian–Taiwan regions, transformed the demographic landscape. Although the Chinese population surpassed the area's Portuguese descendants, it continued to face adversity. Incidents like the rent dispute between the Portuguese Council of Macau and the Qing government (1685–88), the impact of the 1840s Opium Wars, and the comprehensive colonial policies implemented by Governor João Maria Ferreira do Amaral in 1846, deepened the physical and social segregation between the Chinese and their Portuguese masters. These events not only culminated in the eviction of Chinese tenants but also exacerbated xenophobic sentiment. In response, the community came together to establish tight-knit enclaves, demonstrating resilience and putting up a unified front against external pressures.[24] The film's depiction of Sino-Portuguese residents mingling in the streets offers a subtle visual representation of multicultural and religious coexistence. However, this perceived harmony, labelled as performative fusion, only skims the surface, masking the deeper reality of social division and polarization. By the nineteenth century, divisions between the Chinese and Portuguese became more pronounced, such as in the contrasting architectural styles and layouts of the respective communities' living spaces. With its European grandeur and elite villa-style residences, the southern Nam Van region starkly contrasted with the traditional Chinese quarters near the Barrier Gate, Inner Harbour, and central highlands.[25]

In contrast with Adozindo's privileged upbringing, A-Leng comes from the Horta da Mitra district (Check Chai Un), a chevron-shaped neighbourhood located in the heart of the Macau peninsula. The Foc Tac Temple (est. 1886) and its enshrined deities — Fudegong, Mazu, and Caishen — symbolize

---

[24]   Sheng Hua Lou, *Nova História de Macau*, III, p. 873.
[25]   Maria Calado, Maria Clara Mendes, and Michel Toussaint, *Macau, Memorial City on the Estuary of the River of Pearls* (Macau, China: Government of Macau, 1985), pt. 1.

local adherence to Taoist, Buddhist, and indigenous belief systems and their commitment to upholding and preserving ancestral beliefs and values. The temple's vibrant ceremonies, from incense offerings to communal feasts and the distribution of food, are embellished with vibrant opera performances and firework spectacles, but are also used as metaphors for the firecracker, incense, and match industries; while these were crucial in terms of local employment and international trade in the twentieth century, they also epitomized the community's fervent adherence to their cultural identity and societal cohesion in the face of colonialism, especially the Catholic practices of the Portuguese settlers.[26] In the film, the temple is a religious and cultural epicentre that enables the Macanese to cultivate a robust collective sense of belonging; it also offers a sanctuary for those seeking solace and stability, enabling them to embrace their ancestral beliefs and deep-rooted clan values.

At the same time, the temple illustrates the tensions and apprehensions associated with cross-cultural unions, particularly the forbidden romance between the film's main protagonists. The dual role of the temple is framed by the cinematographer both as a haven and a venue for the enactment of punitive measures against those who defy social norms — particularly women who diverge from arranged marriages or consort with Portuguese men. In its examination of the societal repercussions of Adozindo and A-Leng's relationship, the film raises issues concerning notions of marrying outside one's faith (particularly when this involves pagan belief systems), cultural integrity, and social standing. The film delves into the more profound, intangible barriers that govern Macau's social hierarchy. Adozindo's relationship with A-Leng causes him to become involved in a near-fatal brawl, and he attracts the scorn of men who label him as a *gwai lou* [ghost guy]; meanwhile, the ostracism of A-Leng by her foster mother, Queen Bee, underscores intense racial prejudices and the communities' deep-seated resistance to interracial partnerships. The narrative dissects the psyche of Macau's Chinese inhabitants, which has been moulded by the Ming and Qing dynasties' exclusionary policies that barred private commerce and social engagement with foreigners. The harsh imperial penalties for breaching these prohibitions left a lasting impact on the collective consciousness of the Chinese communities in Macau, entrenching a cautious approach towards outsiders.[27] The film skilfully illustrates how these historical policies and legacies have woven themselves into the geographical fabric of the region. Nevertheless, the trajectory of the characters' relationship undergoes a significant metamorphosis, coloured by Adozindo's adopting a tactical approach to exposing A-Leng to his opulent lifestyle and family, and the real-life catastrophe of the 1931 Guia Hill Arsenal explosion.

[26]   Sheng Hua Lou, *Nova História de Macau*, III, p. 871.

[27]   Zhi Hui He, 'Sino-Portuguese Co-Governance in Macao during the Ming and Qing Dynasties' (unpublished doctoral dissertation, Kansai University, 2014), p. 170, doi:10.32286/00000253 [accessed 22 August 2024].

This spatial dichotomy, which became entrenched in the twentieth century, symbolized more than mere physical segregation — it epitomized the deep ideological divides fostered by colonial rule and the predominant influence of Christianity, reflecting Portuguese Macau's historical role as a Catholic missionary hub for Asia, particularly during its time as the *Cidade do Santo Nome de Deus* [City of the Holy Name of God].[28] Furthermore, the intertwining of Catholic traditions with Portugal's cultural and religious expansionism presents the Portuguese as a spiritual and cultural vanguard. Christian spirituality, religious beliefs, and family prestige are exemplified by the Adozindo family's relocation from their initial residence near St Anthony's Church in Camões Square to a mansion near Guia Hill's papal apartments on Vitória Avenue, a move that symbolizes their elevated social standing while hinting at the role played by parochial division and parish affiliation in shaping Macau's administrative and residential landscape. A-Leng's efforts to reintegrate her husband, Adozindo, into the prestigious Portuguese community following the birth of their second son adeptly encapsulate themes such as the Christian ethos of forgiveness and the relentless pursuit of belonging. They highlight the native Macanese community's aspiration to familial harmony and social prestige.

The film also examines the persistence of cultural norms and social paradigms that are ingrained in notions of lineage, honour, and orthodoxy among the native Macanese. This cultural orthodoxy, emphasizing bloodline and noble connections as mechanisms for securing political power, preserved Portuguese and Catholic dominance within a predominantly Chinese environment. Despite state policies such as luso-tropicalism, which were designed to promote assimilation and multicultural integration, the native Macanese resisted miscegenation, driven by their commitment to family honour,[29] while Catholic doctrine prescribed monogamy and upheld the sanctity of marriage as a cornerstone of social order. However, the gender imbalance and the decline of the Portuguese population in Macau created a skewed supply–demand dynamic, significantly inflating the social capital and desirability of single Portuguese men, who found themselves in a position of greater power in marital relationships, facilitating widespread practices of adultery, concubinage, and the proliferation of illegitimate offspring. In this milieu, Eastern women became a focal point in a complex interplay between desire and domination. The film contrasts the treatment of high-class Oriental prostitutes as aesthetic objects of Western men's marital discontent against the idealized Catholic concept of marriage. The director incorporates additional narratives that are not present in the source material to shed more light on the

[28] *Enciclopédia de Macau*, ed. by Zhi Liang Wu and Yun Zhong Yang (Macau: Fundação Macau, 2005), p. 25.
[29] Xue Lian Yan, 'A Study on Macanese Widow Groups in Macao during the Qing Dynasty', *Qing History Journal*, 4 (2022), 81–91 (p. 82).

transient and often exploitative nature of the interactions between Western soldiers and merchants and Eastern women during the colonial era, e.g. the story of Adozindo's father and Queen Bee, along with the heartrending accounts of Portuguese men abandoning pregnant young girls from the Horta da Mitra district and leading them to suicide. The women are positioned at the apex of Western fascination, where they have the status of an inferior otherness within the hierarchical scaffolding of racial and cultural supremacy.[30] These additions touch upon an understudied history.

Phase Two: Race and Socio-Economic Dichotomies

The second phase of the film is characterized by a dissection of the complex interplay of cohabitational struggle, financial woes, cultural and educational disparities, and the gradual dissipation of passion. The original novel delves into the underlying psychological and ideological frameworks that perpetuate the divisions between the communities. Far from being a simplistic portrayal of pagans and deviants, this representation relegates the Chinese inhabitants who are rooted in labour, enduring hardship and striving for sustenance to a symbol of moral degeneration, steeped in misery, shame, and squalor. Their literary portrayal transcends character depiction and becomes a medium for European self-reflection and introspection.

The film portrays the Chinese Horta da Mitra community through the lens of Western Orientalism, wherein it is a realm of decadence, depravity, and enigma.[31] The character traits and daily habits of the principal characters are depicted through the lens of latent Orientalism, that is, unconscious assumptions about the Orient that portray the East as in need of Western enlightenment; e.g. A-Leng's bare feet, her traditional cooking methods, and her burping are regarded by Adozindo as an indication of her cultural inferiority.[32]

Adozindo's self-proclaimed title, the Descendant of the Conqueror, and a lexicon that divides women of British, Portuguese, and Chinese descent into different 'breeds' like specimens in a collection, is part of a dehumanizing and divisive discourse that equates submissiveness with racial inferiority.[33] This is further illustrated by Adozindo's conflicted and eroticized conceptions of the braid; he simultaneously fetishizes exotic symbols of Oriental femininity, chastity, and identity while expressing disdain for A-Leng's cultural practices. The sexual fetishism and objectification of A-Leng's braid are presented as part of the entrenched heteronormative patriarchal–colonial perspective that seeks to fix and normalize eroticism and moral transgressions by shifting the

---

[30]   José I. Suárez, 'Exoticism, Cultural Hybridity, and Subaltern Identity in Three Macanese Novels', *Journal of Lusophone Studies*, 13 (2015), 199–212 (p. 200).
[31]   Said, *Orientalism*, p. 232.
[32]   Said, *Orientalism*, p. 222.
[33]   Senna Fernandes, *The Bewitching Braid*, pp. 21–22.

blame onto Asian women. In *Love and Tiny Toes*, the female Chinese vegetable seller who accompanies Francisco Frontaria on his journey and maturation is portrayed as a vulgar prostitute and servant. Her cohabitation with Francisco symbolizes the man's moral degradation and societal downfall.[34] This dichotomy is repeated in *The Bewitching Braid*, with Adozindo's relationship with A-Leng symbolizing the former's moral decline and rebelliousness.

As the story progresses, the film begins to articulate the dichotomous physical realities of its disparate characters. Adozindo's father holds prominent positions as a government customs officer and shipping magnate while his mother's noble lineage, opulent lifestyle, and busy social calendar point to the family's elevated status within the Macanese community. This perspective is crucial in deconstructing Macau's racial and socio-economic hierarchy in the 1930s, dominated as it was by the Portuguese (and remnants of the British aristocracy). The film sharply contrasts those who are ensconced in privileged socio-economic bastions and who monopolize Macau's administrative, judicial, mercantile, and bureaucratic centres with the Chinese community, many of whom are engaged in manual labour and peripheral enterprises, articulating the divide via the lived experiences of the central characters. It becomes increasingly evident that the racial order, steeped in Orientalist dichotomies and underpinned by Eurocentric and social Darwinist doctrines, goes beyond theoretical constructs to become a manifest reality with profound effects on roles, capital stratification, and social mobility in 1930s Macau.[35] Such Eurocentric presumptions shaped its socio-economic structure, entrenching racial hierarchies, most notably regarding access to social resources. In the film's dichotomous moral universe, Adozindo, despite his transient banishment and subsequent dockside travails, retains the latent social capital inherited from his Lusitanian lineage, facilitating his eventual re-entry into Macau's higher echelons. Adozindo's heritage is both a passport and a form of cultural currency that affords him upward socio-economic mobility, giving him privileges and opportunities unknown to the Chinese populace. By contrast, after her banishment from her community, A-Leng has to sell her braid to subsidize the household; here is a metaphor for colonial subjects teetering toward sexual commodification on account of extreme socio-economic duress. The storyline again underlines the stark structural subjugation endemic to colonial societies and the scarcity of viable livelihood alternatives or pathways for vocational empowerment.

---

[34] Senna Fernandes, *Amor e Dedinhos de Pé: Romance de Macau* (Rio de Janeiro: Gryphus, 2008), pp. 78–79.
[35] Said, *Orientalism*, p. 206.

Phase Three: Gendered Dichotomies:
A Feminized Orient and Dual Marginalization

In the third phase, Adozindo, who feels an increasing sense of responsibility, tolerance, respect, and understanding, legitimizes his union through a Catholic wedding and by kneeling before Queen Bee and asking for her help in delivering his and A-Leng's first child. Despite her being marginalized, A-Leng's tenacity, fortitude, and industriousness play a pivotal role in catalysing Adozindo's transformation, paving the way for a profound shift in the dynamics of their relationship. Against the background of the temple, brilliantly illuminated with red lanterns and candles, Queen Bee emerges as a matriarch whose expertise in areas such as fortune-telling, midwifery, and feng shui demonstrates her significance for the community's well-being.[36] Motherhood is a metaphor for the strategic dominance of the Portuguese colonial regime over Macau's social fabric, effectively supplanting and occupying traditional Chinese patriarchy. The director adeptly incorporates Gayatri Spivak's concept of dual marginalization by juxtaposing two pivotal characters, Aurélio (Adozindo's father) and Queen Bee (A-Leng's adoptive mother).[37] Their existence draws profound historical and socio-cultural parallels between East and West, Portugal and Macau in particular. Queen Bee is depicted as both a victim and a staunch enforcer of clan authority, the enduring power of Manus,[38] and the remnants of the Qing dynasty's feudal system. She prevents European men from having intimate relationships with young Chinese girls; her ideology (where the guardianship of lineage and sexual order is prioritized over personal autonomy) is a manifestation of deeply entrenched patriarchal norms.[39]

By contrast, Aurélio stands for an institutional power that combines political control, theocratic authority, and patriarchy, all augmented and sustained by colonial influence. As a female in a colonial community, A-Leng is subject to a complex web of burdensome Confucian obligations, clan allegiances, moral principles, a strict social code of behaviour for women, racial hegemony, the objectifying colonialist gaze, and class censorship. In the public sphere, Adozindo's lust for conquest is juxtaposed with A-Leng's three consecutive rejections of his advances, including her tactical use of the carrying pole she uses in her job as a waterseller as a tool of physical resistance. In the domestic sphere, A-Leng's lived experience is exacerbated by rigid gender constructions and her subordination to the Confucian ethic of filial piety. The latter, which demands the wife's supreme fidelity and duty to her husband, is vividly realized

---

[36]   *The Bewitching Braid*, dir. by Yuanyuan Cai, 00:22:57–00:24:07.

[37]   Gayatri Chakravorty Spivak, 'Can the Subaltern Speak?', in *Marxism and the Interpretation of Culture*, ed. by Cary Nelson and Lawrence Grossberg (Urbana and Chicago: University of Illinois Press, 1988), pp. 271–313 (p. 283).

[38]   Manus in ancient Roman law was an extreme form of legal control over women within the institution of marriage, institutionalizing male dominance through formal legal structures.

[39]   Gayatri Chakravorty Spivak, *In Other Worlds: Essays in Cultural Politics* (London: Routledge, 2006), p. 135.

in the crucial moments of transformation and in the deeper psychological needs of Adozindo's mind. After Adozindo, who has been scorned by his society, loses his power and prestige, A-Leng willingly and unreservedly serves him in foot-washing rituals and kneeling, providing him with an emotional refuge and pacifying his wounded ego. The boundary between Oriental and Portuguese is made even more unassailable by Adozindo's realization that the special services A-Leng is prepared to provide are intolerable to the pride and status of his Portuguese concubine, Lucrécia, and the other European and American ladies of Macau. A-Leng's submissive gesture is a re-enactment of the colonial dynamic; it not only reinforces Adozindo's authority, inadvertently restoring his lost power and reinforcing self-worth, but also compensates for his rejection, affirming his decision to deviate from his normative community lifestyle.

The film portrays Adozindo's eroticized conceptions and fetishistic views of Asian women's braids as part of a broader discourse that devalues and appropriates Oriental culture. The director uses full-frame shots and a centre-framing of the braid to signal the colonialists' insatiable gaze for dominion over indigenous resources, bodies, and identities.[40] It is also employed as a means of exploring the unfamiliar territory of Eastern aesthetics in an accessible way. Adozindo's bold Western advances and passionate ways of expressing his wish to possess A-Leng's braid are signifiers of the colonizer's emotions of reclaiming, appropriating, and remaking their subjects. This dynamic resonates with Adozindo's profound disquietude and regret regarding the possibility of Chinese women marrying local men — along with the implications for their descendants that entails — and lays bare the so-called cultural arrogance embedded in the colonial system, one that places their matrimonial choices, relational determinations, and socio-cultural norms at the top of the racial and gender hierarchy. It also permeates the intimate spheres of reproductive rights, sexuality, and familial structures.[41] The decision to name the three main female characters — A-Leng, A-Sôi, and A Abelha-Mestra [Queen Bee] — without legitimate family names emphasizes their marginalization and the colonial erasure of their indigenous identities. In Chinese culture, the prefix A denotes endearment or familiarity, akin to 'little' or 'dear', but also reduces identity to a generic and non-specific level, signifying a loss of genealogical roots in a social context that values family relations inherited from ancestry and patrilineal descent. In the colonial context of Macau, the nomenclature marks a profound de-identification and lack of individual recognition. A similar theme is explored in Love and Tiny Toes, when Francisco Frontaria has the braids of three Chinese men tied together in the public Largo do Pagode do Bazar near the Templo de Hong Chan Kuan.[42] The public nature of this act and its subsequent widespread anecdotal dissemination in the diocese suggest that it

40 The Bewitching Braid, dir. by Yuanyuan Cai, 00:18:04–00:18:17, 01:31:33–01:32:02.
41 Michel Foucault, The History of Sexuality: An Introduction (New York: Vintage Books, 1981), p. 108.
42 Senna Fernandes, Amor e Dedinhos de Pé, pp. 24–25.

was not a mere act of mischief but rather a performative display of Portuguese power and domination.

The braid is initially devalued and ridiculed, then its elements are exoticized and appropriated to satisfy Western desires. In Asian cultures, the transformation of a young girl's braid to chignon after marriage marks a rite of passage, signifying a shift from youth to marital commitment and reflecting social norms, life transitions, and personal identity, as well as accentuating the constraints on female morality and agency imposed by Confucian marriage customs. Adozindo's obsession with the braid signifies his internalized purity, chastity, and fidelity to Oriental women. This is particularly evident when Adozindo faces the implication that A-Leng's sale of her braid symbolically suggests a descent into prostitution — a subtle innuendo in the original novel that the film renders explicit. After A-Leng angrily threatens to sell her braid to contribute to the household expenses and storms out, Adozindo frantically searches for her. Therefore, encountering another A-Leng with similar braids triggers Adozindo's deep-seated fears and insecurities, demonstrating his desperation to retain his idea of the idealized traditional Oriental woman. Such is the complex interplay between desire, greed, and colonial nostalgia. Later, Adozindo's emotional turmoil is vividly portrayed through his tears and reaction upon seeing A-Leng's braid intact before he realizes it is her. If maintaining a single physical trait becomes the key to sustaining a relationship, then the depth and authenticity of that connection must be questioned. By distilling the richness and complexity of A-Leng's cultural identity into a single, symbolic representation, her qualities of toughness, self-reliance, and determination are eclipsed by Adozindo's Orientalist gaze. This fits neatly into Said's Orientalist framework, wherein the West tends to reduce the East to consumable, exotic fragments while ignoring the depth and richness of its cultures.[43]

Auditory Dichotomies

The auditory landscape in *The Bewitching Braid* delineates cultural boundaries and identities. The masterly soundtrack was sculpted by renowned Brazilian conductor Veiga Jardim. Collaborating closely with the director, Jardim's sonic choices function as an intricate counterpoint, amplifying and deepening the visual dichotomies so meticulously presented on screen. The use of the Portuguese guitar — a resonant instrument deeply embedded in the *Fado* tradition of longing and melancholy — essentializes the character of Adozindo and acts as an aural representation of the West's romanticized and intricate ties to colonial Macau. Contrarily, A-Leng's character is bathed in melodies drawn from Chinese pentatonic scales, rendered evocatively through instruments like

---

[43] Said, *Orientalism*, pp. 128, 177–79.

the Dizi, Er-hu, Pipa, and Guzheng.[44] The Western musical motifs (waltzes for Lucrécia and Florêncio) and Chinese folk-inspired melodies for A-Leng and Queen Bee amplify the tension between the exotic allure of the East and the refined sensibilities of the West.[45]

On the other hand, the synthesis of Adozindo and A-Leng's musical themes into a concerto for piano and orchestra during the wedding scene is a departure from stereotypical binaries, suggesting a metaphorical representation of the blending of two worlds and alluding to the possibility of new identities birthed from the interplay of colonial histories and native traditions.[46] This deliberate musical differentiation aesthetically demarcates the characters and complements and elevates the film's visual dichotomies.

A Palimpsestic Approach to Directing

The film adaptation unravels the complexities and contradictions inherent in Macau's societal fabric, deconstructs the cultural myth of a harmonious and racially integrated society, and opens up spaces for further critiques. In the 1990s, with the imminent transfer of Macau's sovereignty from Portugal to China, the Beijing government carefully cultivated a cohesive national narrative, orchestrating the process through a variety of media outlets and catapulting the small city from the geopolitical periphery to the cultural and political centre. In the meantime, China's film distribution system, which was placed on a market-orientated footing in 1994, positioned Macau as a Golconda for filmmakers and investors. The Cai brothers, mainland filmmakers, and investors were eager to capitalize on Macau cinema's under-exploited themes and national strategies for commercial gain. Their subsequent production of Senna Fernandes's novel (in collaboration with the Zhujiang Film Studio Company and the China Film Co-Production Corporation) assumed a seminal position in Sino-Portuguese cinema. The Beijing government lauded them as pioneers, an endorsement that assured them of a role in soft diplomacy; e.g. the film was formally presented to Jorge Sampaio, then President of Portugal.[47] However, the degree of Sino-Portuguese cooperation appears to have been exaggerated. The chairman, general manager, and deputy manager of the film's central production entity (the Cai Brothers (Macau) Film Co. Ltd) are Chinese nationals who migrated to Portuguese Macau from the mainland in 1989.[48] As such, the collaborative

[44] Rogério Luz, 'A Trança Feiticeira — o Filme do Romance de Henrique de Senna Fernandes em, CD da Trilha Sonora e Livro', *Cronicas Macaenses*, 2022 <https://wp.me/pWGo3-a8t> [accessed 22 August 2024].
[45] Veiga Jardim, 'Track 8: Ju Po's Tale', 'Track 9: A-Leng's Tale', 'Track 10: Old Waltz (Lucrécia's Theme)', *The Soundtrack Album of The Bewitching Braid / A Trança Feiticeira* (PhonoArt, 1996).
[46] Jardim, 'Track 17: Adozindo Marries A-Leng (Wedding March)'.
[47] Xiaozheng Geng, 'Cai An-an's Dream of Macaense Movie', *Macau Inc*, 11 (2013), 30–33.
[48] In Macau, the Cai brothers were recognized and registered under their Cantonese names: Choi On-on and Choi Yunyun.

nature of the production may be regarded as a strategic gimmick to secure policy support and capital. The brothers were instrumental in creating the film project; they were the primary scriptwriters, with the older of the two (Yuanyuan Cai) taking on the directorial mantle. Their initial ventures in the Shenzhen Special Economic Zone and Zhuhai were met with a complex web of bureaucratic challenges. However, the comparatively liberal environment of Macau in the late 1980s encouraged artistic freedom and private enterprise, which aligned with their cinematic ambitions; the relocation to Macau and the founding of the Cai Brothers (Macau) Film Co. Ltd in 1989, allowed Macau's first significant film to be made. Cai An-an strategically engaged mainland stakeholders at the 1994 Beijing film distribution marketization conference, and his advocacy led to the staging of an investment fair in Macau, attracting investments ranging from 150,000 yuan to one million yuan.[49] The combination of colonial themes with emergent national narratives contributed significantly to the film's artistic acclaim and socio-political resonance. However, hindered by the lack of star power, outdated theatre management, and inefficient revenue sharing, Macau's fledging movie industry fell into a decade-long hiatus.[50] The director's need to mortgage his house and the film's low return highlight systemic financial challenges in Macau's film industry, including the seizure of Cai Brothers' company assets.

The Cai brothers' endeavours highlighted the dilemmas and limitations inherent in filmmaking at the confluence of diverse cultural identities and national agendas. Coming from a family deeply involved in cinema and theatre, and as child actors involved in several well-known revolutionary and anti-Japanese films financed by state agencies, the brothers were heavily indoctrinated by state-sanctioned narratives from an early age. They went on to accumulate cultural capital and extensive experience in state-controlled cinematic production and television broadcasting institutions and established China's first private film and television production company in 1985. They later established solid interpersonal and social relations by collaborating with the National Film Studio and National Television in producing the first Sino-Macanese film *The Night Robbery* (1989).[51] These experiences made the brothers aware that local narratives and various literary and artistic creation themes must be actively aligned with the country's overarching socio-political agenda. These diverse influences are evident in their approach to the adaptation of *The Bewitching Braid*. The brothers' sensitivity and awareness of political and cultural nuances, rooted in their personal histories and the socio-political context of Macau's impending return to Beijing, guided the decision to subtly alter the original novel's Orientalist narrative and systematic bias and avoid any

---

[49] Associação de Filme e Televisão de Macau, 'The Difficulty of Starting a Business: Private Film and Television Pioneer Cai An-an in His Own Words', *Associação de Filme e Televisão de Macau* (Macau, 2012) [accessed 22 August 2024].
[50] Ricardo Carriço and Ning Jing, prominent actors, portrayed Adozindo and A-Leng respectively.
[51] Associação de Filme e Televisão de Macau, 'The Difficulty of Starting a Business'.

debates on Macanese politics and identity.[52] The novel's three-part structure was altered significantly. The first two sections, which focus on the protagonists' encounters and challenges before their marriage, are retained, but the third one, depicting A-Leng's transition from the Horta da Mitra community to a more elevated socio-economic position, is conspicuously absent. Key elements such as A-Leng's adoption of Portuguese customs and language, and Catholicism, each representing her assimilation into Portuguese-Macanese society, are omitted.[53] The decision to censor this part of the narrative accorded with the timing of the film's release, i.e. the eve of Macau's handover to China. A-Leng's abandonment of her Chinese roots might have conflicted with the prevailing sentiments on the mainland, where sovereignty and national identity were contentious issues. The demise of Queen Bee, which the director added, marks a significant turning point in A-Leng's journey; it acts as a metaphor for the weakening of A-Leng's Chinese identity, thus avoiding the possibility that mainland audiences might view her trajectory as symbolizing the loss of Macau's cultural identity as a Portuguese colony.[54]

Similarly, the brothers downplayed the sense of hostility, ambivalence, and aversion between the Portuguese upper class and the local Chinese community but consequently diluted the novel's artistry in exploring intercultural relationships. This self-censorship reflected the era's anxieties and the Cai brothers' professional experience, which had been characterized by a continual interplay between state-dominated artistic paradigms and market incentives. The brothers' use of Mandarin and Portuguese expanded the potential audience and aligned with Beijing's policy of promoting Mandarin as the national *lingua franca*. Their engagement in state-influenced art forms had taught them to privilege cohesion over regional or subcultural identities. However, marginalization, a vital element of Macau's cultural and linguistic identity, might have been construed as a form of cultural erasure, subtly undermining the region's unique heritage. The choice of language (or the absence of Cantonese and Macanese Patois) represented a significant instance of cultural erasure, diminishing the intricate tapestry of Macau's historical richness and the multifaceted nature of its contemporary linguistic state. The decision was not just a marketing strategy, catering to the needs of a more extensive consumer base on mainland China; it also reflected the director's involvement in state-run film studios. In short, the brothers' artistic paradigm was, therefore, entwined with broader socio-political and economic factors.

The parts of the original novel leaning towards Western values and providing a balanced interpretative framework were reconstructed. Senna Fernandes's portrayal of Western weddings as lavish (in stark contrast to the modest traditional Chinese wedding ceremony) was given a significant makeover.[55] The

---

[52] Senna Fernandes, *The Bewitching Braid*, pp. 24–26.
[53] Senna Fernandes, *The Bewitching Braid*, chap. 28.
[54] *The Bewitching Braid*, dir. by Yuanyuan Cai, 01:41:54–01:43:07.
[55] Senna Fernandes, *The Bewitching Braid*, chap. 22.

film contains a traditional Chinese celebration of a baby's reaching one month of age, elevating the event to match the opulence of the Western-style wedding, thereby addressing and rectifying the novel's narrative imbalance. Central to the wedding scene is the poignant moment when A-Leng, habitually barefoot, discards her uncomfortable high heels and Adozindo takes off his leather shoes. This barefoot solidarity shows the newlyweds discarding preconceived notions and societal expectations as part of a bold step towards authentic self-expression, vanquishing cultural divides, and embracing a shared humanity. Cai's directorial approach respects the integrity of the original narrative and enhances it with contemporary insights and perspectives. A-Leng's initial hesitation to embrace modern medical assistance, which stems from deep-rooted traditional values, makes Adozindo's decision to transcend his own cultural biases and seek help from Queen Bee into a moving cinematic moment, symbolizing the couple's journey towards understanding and acceptance.[56]

Indeed, this is the narrative kernel of the film — an authentic dialogue between Eastern and Western cultures, advocating mutual respect and understanding between different paradigms for the sake of pluralistic and coexistent interaction. This recalibration not only alters the tone and structure of the narrative but also shifts the film's focus from a monolithic Orientalist perspective to one emphasizing agency. A-Leng evolves from an Orientalist archetype of a humble, vulgar, and traditional woman to a character embodying resilience, assertiveness, and empowerment. Her departure from conventional educational norms represents a form of adaptive intellectualism characterized by an autodidactic spirit. Her refusal to be bribed and her participation in the male-dominated lion dance represent a departure from conventional gender roles and the evolution of societal attitudes towards race, gender, and the concept of otherness. These narrative choices humanize the Oriental characters, stress the importance of defying colonial societal constraints and Chinese socio-political agency, and subtly affirm anti-colonial and nationalist sentiments. This cinematic recalibration culminates in the film's climax — the birth of the married couple's mixed-race child and the subsequent acceptance of the protagonists back into their respective communities.[57] The director thereby crafts a tableau of cultural amalgamation and allegorizes the potential for the resolution of tensions during the Sino-Portuguese transition. In a union fraught with cultural misunderstandings and difference, the braid's stark visibility and tactility provide a tangible anchor for the tumultuous relationship between the two principal characters, serving as a silent arbiter of its evolution. It is imbued with anxiety, mutual commitment, and shared beliefs, bridging two different worlds. Through this skilful melding of Sino-Portuguese elements, the Cai brothers' adaptation gives oriental characters an uncommon depth and humanity, liberating them from one-dimensional portrayals and taking

[56]   *The Bewitching Braid*, dir. by Yuanyuan Cai, 01:34:04–01:35:37.
[57]   *The Bewitching Braid*, dir. by Yuanyuan Cai, 01:43:11–01:47:07.

the audience on an immersive journey through Macau's evolving social and cultural landscape.

Conclusion

The Bewitching Braid represents a profound engagement with Macau's colonial legacy and the intricate dynamics of Sino-Portuguese identity. In the film, Senna Fernandes's literary work, deeply entrenched in Orientalist perspectives, is subtly reconfigured to reflect an evolving socio-political landscape and the nuanced interplay of tradition and modernity. The film does more than tell a story; it is a palimpsest that critically deconstructs colonial domination and the ideological framework of Orientalism. The storyline is an exploration of the complex intercultural symbiosis of Senna Fernandes's portrayal of the gradual dissolution of rigid ethnocultural boundaries and the director's visual acuity. The film adaptation, while maintaining aspects of Oriental exoticism, stresses the need for integration. The brothers' nuanced approach, balancing Orientalist traditions with political sensitivities, mirrors the shifting socio-cultural rifts between the Chinese and Portuguese communities. The film's critical and complex deconstruction of the Orientalist perspective marks a significant evolution in Macau's cinematic landscape, reflecting broader shifts in post-colonial identity and social perceptions in the late twentieth century. *The Bewitching Braid* and its film adaptation challenge entrenched narratives and call for an equitable egalitarian understanding of Macau's rich cultural and historical tapestry. The present study has illuminated the delicate nexus between colonial history, power dynamics, and the enduring impact of Orientalism, emphasizing the transformative power of cinema in redefining cultural narratives and identities.

'Portuguese India':
Between the Desire for a Konkani Cinema
and the Paradoxes of Filmed Propaganda

MARIA DO CARMO PIÇARRA

Lisbon (ICNOVA-FCSH)

The Estado Novo (1933–74) shifted to Africa the nostalgic image of the mythology of greatness (transversal to several administrations) surrounding the 'Portuguese Orient' — projected by the dictatorship as an illustration of the 'Portuguese way of being in the world' and the place where the professed merit of Lusitanian colonialization materialized. To overcome Portugal's geographical smallness, and the scarcity of human, economic and technological resources, a historical right to own colonies was declared, reclaiming the primacy of maritime expansion and the supposed specificity of a colonialism sustained by a Christian 'civilizing' mission, promoted by the cinema. Before the constitution was passed, in 1933, the dictatorship had already defined a civilizational hierarchy, regulated by the 1930 *Acto Colonial e do Estatuto Político, Civil e Criminal dos Indígenas* [Colonial Act and Political, Civil and Criminal Statute of the Indigenous Subject]. Implicitly racist, this act differentiated between the rights and duties of those born in the metropolis and those native to the colonies, lessening the latter. In this pyramidal society, the bottom was made up of Angolans, Mozambicans, and Guineans; with the Timorese and Santomeans in the middle, and the Indians, Macanese, and Cape Verdeans nearer the top.[1]

Despite the regime's valorization of the cinema as a tool, a dearth is still felt today, in Portugal, with regards to studies about how the colonies were portrayed in film, and the political and ideological changes that took place during this colonial tenure[2] — the equating of 'Empire' with 'African Empire' is also common. Thus, the study of how the 'Portuguese Orient' is

---

[1] Patrícia Ferraz de Matos, *As Cores do Império* (Lisbon: Imprensa de Ciências Sociais, 2006), p. 66.

[2] The study of filmic representations of colonialism started with *O Cinema Sob o Olhar de Salazar*, ed. by Luís Reis Torgal (Lisbon: Temas e Debates, 2000), in which, in 'Imagens do Império' (pp. 235–73), Jorge Seabra examines the film *Chaimite* (1953), by Jorge Brum do Canto. However, both in the referred chapter and in Seabra's doctoral thesis, *África Nossa*, 2nd edn (Coimbra: Imprensa da Universidade de Coimbra, 2014), a correspondence is made between colonial empire and Africa, notwithstanding the fact that they also focus on *Amor e Dedinhos de Pé* [Love and Tiny Toes] (1992), shot by Luís Filipe Rocha in Macau.

Portuguese Studies vol. 40 no. 2 (2024), doi:10.1353/port.00012, pp. 142–58
© Modern Humanities Research Association 2024

represented in film is still embryonic.[3] That the territories that come under the designation 'Portuguese Orient' are diverse is but a given. This implies that a characterization of each territory's specific representation in film is made, by means of examining and listing the relevant Portuguese filmography and surveying the documentation relating to its production. This essay focuses on the case of the former 'Portuguese India'.

Orientalism in Film

Building upon what he had formulated in *Orientalism*, where he saw the corpus of works about the Orient as a single discourse, in *Culture and Imperialism* Edward Said looked to the literary text to elucidate the dynamics of politics and culture in relation to imperialism.[4] Said contended that it is through culture that imperialism is 'legitimized' and proceeds to impose its economic model. He surveyed a wealth of 'orientalist' narratives to show how language, images and symbols bear a formative, and not merely expressive, nature, moulding identities, and the imagination, subjectivity, history, culture, and interactions that exist between those who oppress and those who are oppressed. He concluded that these images shaped the West's negative conception of the 'other' and justified its 'obligation' to dominate.

Few studies exist in Portugal about the representation of former eastern colonies in film. I evoke Said in support of the kind of analysis that is proposed here, where I argue that the Estado Novo's ideology concerning the 'Portuguese Orient' also made an impact on Portuguese film discourse. As Jean-Michel Frodon proposes, the nation shares with the cinema the requirement to project itself in order to exist.[5] In *La Projection nacionale*, Frodon asserts that the cinema arose in the twentieth century as a producer of mythologies beyond the need to provide contentment to the masses. Drawing on Benedict Anderson's conception of the nation as 'an imagined political community — and imagined as both inherently limited and sovereign',[6] Frodon emphasizes that both the cinema and the nation can only exist by way of projection. According to him, the nation is an invention that is constantly being revised and corrected against a dramaturgy. He also maintains that the criteria that define the nation also apply to the cinema. The cinema is, for Frodon, the projection of a trace of

---

[3] 'Oriente Português': 'que se estrutura num período que decorre dos primeiros anos do século XVI até às primeiras décadas do século XVIII, termo temporal em que se pode considerar estabilizado o processo de estabelecimento do Estado português no Oriente' ['Portuguese Orient': which is structured during a period between the first years of the sixteenth century and the first decades of the eighteenth century, a temporal term in the course of which the process of establishing the Portuguese State in the Orient can be considered stabilized]. António Vasconcelos de Saldanha, *Iustum Imperium: dos tratados como fundamento do Império dos Portugueses no Oriente* (Lisbon: Instituto Superior de Ciências Sociais e Políticas, Universidade Técnica de Lisboa, 2004), p. 28.

[4] Edward Said, *Culture and Imperialism* (New York: Knopf, 1993).

[5] Jean-Michel Frodon, *La Projection nationale: cinéma et nation* (Paris: Odile Jacob, 1998).

[6] Benedict Anderson, *Imagined Communities* (London: Verso, 1983), p. 6.

reality, and this differentiates it from previous comparable techniques. This projection is enacted on a large scale, in the dark, before a spectatorship sharing a single 'magnified view'.

In *Visions of the East: Orientalism in Film*, Matthew Bernstein and Gaylyn Studlar discuss how the imaginaries generated by literary orientalism have been transposed to film.[7] Film inherited both orientalism's disseminated cultural assumptions and its narrative and visual languages. Thus, cinematic orientalism became instantly popular, with major orientalist films being produced in France and the USA as early as the silent film era, forming an imaginary that remained widespread throughout the century.

Despite the common use of the expression 'Portuguese Orient' during the Estado Novo dictatorship, few films about the former eastern colonies were produced. Besides the fact that film production in and about Portugal's eastern colonies — mainly documentaries, the dictatorship's favourite means of propaganda — was late and scarce, there is also a contemporary dearth of academic study focused on the Orientalism presented in these works.

In *Tradition, Culture and Aesthetics in Contemporary Asian Cinema*, Peter Pugsley notes that, for many an author, Orientalism remains alive.[8] He underscores the importance of a type of research focused on cinematic Orientalism that transcends superficial analysis, and constantly searches for traces of the suppression of alterity and detects where this alterity becomes noticeable.

The Orient's Symbolic Value and the Pioneering Spirit of Colonial Film Propaganda

If Orientalism was less valued in Portugal, during the Romantic period, between the second half of the nineteenth century and the first half of the twentieth, than in other European countries, the Portuguese orientalists still reveal, according to Marta Pacheco Pinto, 'an almost fetishistic obsession with the history of Portuguese presence in the Orient'.[9] The 'Portuguese Orient', which, during the twentieth century, was limited to 'Portuguese India' (Goa, Daman, Diu, Dadra, and Nagar Haveli), besides Macau and Portuguese Timor, retained little more than a symbolic value. This loss of status of the Portuguese presence in the Orient was first offset by a relaying of grandeur to the control of Brazil. And when Brazil became independent, in 1822, this was further conveyed to Angola and Mozambique.

---

[7]   Matthew Bernstein and Gaylyn Studlar, *Visions of the East: Orientalism in Film* (New Brunswick, NJ: Rutgers University Press, 1997).

[8]   Peter C. Pugsley, *Tradition, Culture and Aesthetics in Contemporary Asian Cinema* (London: Taylor & Francis, 2013).

[9]   Marta Pacheco Pinto, 'Orientalismo', in *Dicionário de Historiadores Portugueses: da Academia Real das Ciências ao final do Estado Novo* (Lisbon: Biblioteca Nacional de Portugal, 2022) <https://dichp. bnportugal.gov.pt/imagens/orientalismo.pdf> [accessed 15 March 2022].

As Sérgio Campos Matos highlights, it was during the Constitutional Monarchy that a few intellectual voices started to question the possession of the eastern colonies, given their limited impact on the national economy.[10] My hypothesis is that the symbolic value of the Orient was nurtured by a certain vagueness in the propaganda — which superficially evoked the allegedly specific characteristics of local socio-cultural experiences forged in miscegenation, through a 'shared' history, projected by the films about the territories in the region.

The emergence of the Estado Novo crowned the transition to authoritarianism launched by the military coup of 28 May 1926. To gain legitimacy, it developed a nationalist ideology, incorporating a political view about the colonies that was disseminated by the cinema, amongst other channels. The President of the Council, Oliveira Salazar (1933–68), rested the responsibility for 'projecting' the nation through culture on António Ferro. As Director of the *Secretariado da Propaganda Nacional* (SNP) [National Secretariat of Propaganda], António Ferro stylized traditional culture and promoted historical revisionism.[11]

How was the dictatorship's ideology then projected by the cinema? With the immediate financing of filmed propaganda and nationalistic films. Nevertheless, only in 1948 do we witness the creation of the *Fundo Nacional do Cinema* (FNC) [National Film Fund], which defined the cinematic model to be enforced subsequently. To benefit from the support of the State, films should 'ser representativo do espírito português, que traduza a psicologia, os costumes, as tradições, a história, a alma colectiva do povo' [be representative of the Portuguese spirit, which expresses the psychology, the customs, traditions, history, collective soul of the people].[12]

Up to the dawn of the so-called colonial war, which started in Angola in 1961 and spread to Guinea-Bissau and Mozambique, until it stabilized in these three countries around 1964,[13] little about the colonies was shown in film, apart from two film missions promoted at the end of the 1920s and 1930s, for political reasons.

The documentary was the genre most used to propagandize colonialism. Colonial policy was still being drafted when the *Agência Geral das Colónias* (AGC) [General Agency of the Colonies], created in 1925, sent two teams to film in the African colonies, but no films were made in either Cape Verde or the Portuguese Orient. Productions depicting Angola, Mozambique, Guinea and São Tomé and Príncipe were exhibited at the Ibero-American Exposition in Seville (1929), the International Exposition for Colonies, Maritime Affairs

[10] Sérgio Campos Matos, 'Oriente e Orientalismo em Portugal no século XIX: o caso de Oliveira Martins', in *Cadmo*, 12 (Lisbon: Instituto Oriental da Universidade de Lisboa, 2002), pp. 211–24.
[11] Created in 1933 and refashioned as the *Secretariado Nacional da Informação* (SNI) [National Secretariat of Information] in 1944.
[12] Law 2027, of 18 February 1948.
[13] The war continued in Angola, Mozambique, and Guinea-Bissau until the Revolution of 25 April 1974 (led by a group of low-ranking officers displeased with the situation) put an immediate stop to it.

and Flemish Art in Antwerp (1930) and the Paris Colonial Exposition (1931). The Antwerp Exposition also showcased an amateur film about Goa made by Antunes Amor.

In addition to one-off productions, the emergence of sound in film led to the Cinematographic Mission to the African Colonies of 1938. However, the Asian territories were once again excluded. Following the Second World War, with the outbreak of independence movements against European colonialism, the Portuguese government still managed to integrate the country into the Marshall Plan recovery programme, despite not having participated in the war. In this context, the economic documentary rose in importance, on the initiative of Felipe Solms and Ricardo Malheiro, who travelled to Mozambique and Angola in 1949 to raise funds to produce films for companies, State agencies and religious missions.

Upon taking the role of Minister, in 1950, Sarmento Rodrigues put into motion an administrative and ideological reform of the politico-colonial model. He adopted Luso-tropicalism, a concept developed by the sociologist Gilberto Freyre, which proposed the unique adaptability of the Portuguese and their culture to tropical locales.[14] According to Freyre, Portugal, Brazil, Africa, and the Portuguese Orient constituted a whole, a group with a shared 'unity of sentiment and culture',[15] and a tendency towards miscegenation. These commonalities were supposedly grounded in Christianity and this idea became a common defence used by the dictatorship in response to the international scrutiny of its continued ruling over the colonies.

Only with the onset of the Portuguese dispute with newly independent India,[16] did the propaganda film turn its attention eastwards. Orientalism was, by then, subordinate to a Luso-tropicalist rhetoric propelled by film. Based on the historical revisionism introduced in the nineteenth century and developed by Ferro as Director of Propaganda, the 'Luso-orientalism' conveyed by film emerged when Freyre's Luso-tropicalist 'theory' was adopted by the dictatorship. It incorporated discursive elaborations concerning both the specificities of Portugal's colonization of its territories and the threats to Portuguese sovereignty in each. These 'Luso-oriental' films called attention to

[14] Freyre used the expression Luso-tropicalism in November of 1951, at a conference in Goa, on a trip at the invitation of Sarmento Rodrigues. The concept was later developed in *Aventura e Rotina* [Adventure and Routine] and *Um Brasileiro em Terras Portuguesas* [A Brazilian in Portuguese Lands]. Gilberto Freyre, *Um Brasileiro em Terras Portuguêsas: Introdução a Uma Possível Luso-tropicologia, Acompanhada de Conferências e Discursos Proferidos em Portugal e em Terras Lusitanas e ex-Lusitanas da Ásia, da África e do Atlântico* (Lisbon: Edição Livros do Brasil, 1953); Gilberto Freyre, *Aventura e Rotina* (Lisbon: Livros do Brasil, 1962).

[15] Freyre, *Aventura e Rotina*, p. 267.

[16] Franco Nogueira, Minister of Foreign Affairs (1961–68) during the dictatorship, characterized Indian politics, beginning in 1947, as having advanced with phases of political pressure, intimidation, and international debate. In 1953, India accused the Estado Novo of pursuing a 'policy of violent repression' and called for the transfer of sovereignty. The Portuguese response was uncompromising. On 11 June of that same year, India withdrew its diplomatic mission from Lisbon. According to Nogueira, a phase of intimidation had begun. Franco Nogueira, *O Estado Novo (1933–1974)* (Porto: Livraria Civilização Editora, 1981).

a range of issues: military and 'scientific' matters in Timor; martial and political affairs in Portuguese India; and political, economic, and touristic concerns in Macau.

In 1952, Ricardo Malheiro, hired by the *Agência Geral do Ultramar* (AGU)[17] [General Overseas Agency], escorted the Overseas Minister, Sarmento Rodrigues, on a tour of the Orient. Malheiro revived the financial model used in Africa, proposing propaganda films to private companies and local administrations. Soon after, Miguel Spiguel also started making propaganda films.

Sarmento Rodrigues, a minister since 1950, had elicited an administrative reform that did not neglect the ideological remodelling of the colonial-political model. He adapted Gilberto Freyre's (pseudo-)theory, which asserted a supposed multiculturalism rooted in the specific adaptability of the Portuguese and their culture to tropical settings. In August 1951, only two months after a constitutional review that included ideological adjustments with terminological implications — the word 'colonies' was replaced by 'overseas', to assert territorial continuity — Freyre was invited by Rodrigues to embark on a tour of Portugal and the 'Portuguese overseas world'. It was during that journey that he used the expression *Luso-tropicalism* for the first time, on the occasion of a talk in Goa, and in *Aventura e Rotina* he asserts that, through observation, he has verified the existence of a Luso-tropical community. Portugal, Brazil, Africa, and the Portuguese Orient constituted, according to Freyre, a 'unity of meaning and culture',[18] within a tendency for miscegenation, and this unity has been sustained by Christianity.

When, in 1961, the struggle for liberation broke out in Angola, the regime intensified the use of a Luso-tropicalist rhetoric, above all in the context of foreign affairs and in response to international questioning vis-à-vis the perpetuation of the colonies. The regime invested also in the production and exhibition of propaganda films, both to overcome a profound ignorance about the colonies and their peoples, and to reaffirm the alleged specificity the metropolis had in its relationship with its 'overseas provinces'. That the 'Portuguese Orient' suddenly becomes a subject ripe for filming resulted from the need to cement a Luso-orientalist discourse, which, abstracted from local reality and the differences between each African or Asian territory, seeks to avow, against all evidence, that 'from Minho to Timor we are all Portuguese', an expression popularized at the time.

However, given the outcome of the 'Goa question' — which culminated with the annexation of 'Portuguese India' by India in December 1961 — and the political and symbolic importance of the loss of these territories, it is remarkable how little prominence the Orient had in the production of propaganda films. The lack of interest can be partially justified by the great land distance between these territories and mainland Portugal, their scant contribution to the

[17] Designation given to the former AGC, after the constitutional revision of 1951. 'Overseas' officially replaces 'colonies'.
[18] Freyre, *Aventura e Rotina*, p. 267.

economy, and their small size compared to Angola and Mozambique. However, the region retained symbolic and political importance, as the dictatorship kept promoting nationalistic values founded on the past grandeur of the Portuguese Orient, now projected onto Africa, while also enlisting the Orient as historical justification for its right to maintain an empire. In fact, the Portuguese presence in inland Africa remained limited until the twentieth century, due to fear of tropical disease, combined with the fragility of the Portuguese army and economy. Thus, it was paramount that the importance of empire was buoyed by an evocation of fifteenth-century maritime expansion.

Regardless of its past importance in the history of Portugal, when the Orient was finally filmed, both image and voiceover were subordinated to propaganda and determined by political events, ignoring local realities.

The Making and Screening of Films in India and Goa

The first ever screening in India — featuring films by the Lumière brothers — took place on 7 July 1896, in Bombay (Mumbai), at the Watson's Hotel. One of the attendees, photographer Harishchandra Sakharam Bhatavdekar, later known as Save Dada, became the first Indian national to make a motion film, having imported a camera from London, with which he registered a fight and aspects of day-to-day life in the city. It was only in 1913 that the first Indian feature, *Raja Harishchandra*, was filmed, produced by Dada Saheb Phalke; it was a colossal hit. In the 1920s, Bombay (Mumbai) and Calcutta (Kolkata) became the largest centres in India for film production. Among the female silent film stars of the time, Ermelinda Cardoso, a Goan who was raised illiterate on the island of Divar and then moved to Bombay with her underprivileged family, made her debut in 1925, age seventeen, and became known as Sudhabala. The transition to sound film put an end to Sudhabala's career — she would have spoken a deeply popular Hindi — but not without first gaining public notoriety for repelling sexual harassment. When the cinematographer Chaturbai Patel and the director Khanjibhai Rathod forced entry into her room, during a shooting, she brought charges against both, but was disfavoured by the judge for being an actress and of Goan origins. However, Sudhabala never gave up and she eventually won her case.

The impact of Goa in Indian cinema derived mostly from the presence of Goan musicians and composers active in the industry, especially after 1931. However, film screening in Goa did not happen immediately, with the date of the first session still unknown. According to Gautam Kaul, 'The mother country, Portugal, was still just above the poverty level, and colonial enterprise was still limited to mining for minerals and cultivation of traditional cash crops like cashew nuts and mangoes'.[19]

---

[19]   Gautam Kaul, 'A Brief History of Konkani Cinema', *Film Critics Circle*, 15 October 2019, <https://filmcriticscircle.com/journal/all/a-brief-history-of-konkani-cinema/>.

The first silent film to be shot and screened in Goa was titled *Os Brahamanes* [The Brahmins]. It was an adaptation to the screen of the homonymous novel written in 1866 by Francisco Luís Gomes — the first Goan novel in Portuguese. The production, by the Kahinoor Film Co. from Bombay, was approved by the Portuguese Governor. The film premiered in Goa on 25 November 1929.

Before the 1920s, only one cinema existed, the *Éden*, in Panjim (Panaji), on the spot which is now occupied by the city council. Reacting to the popularity of sound film — which had an enormous impact on the development of the Indian film industry from 1931 onwards — on 25 November 1934 a purpose-built cinema was inaugurated on a plot owned by the municipality.[20] It was the *Cine Teatro Nacional*, run under contract by Roulú and Esvonra Volvonta Rau, tradespeople who had previously owned the *Éden*. It was an attractive building, opened by Governor João Carlos Craveiro Lopes just prior to the screening of *The Kid from Spain* (Leo McCarey, 1932), a musical comedy starring Eddie Cantor. The second film was *Sky Devils* (Edward Sutherland, 1932), which stars Spencer Tracy playing a deserter who can never escape the war.

Throughout its life, the *Nacional* privileged the exhibition of Indian and Hollywood productions.[21] During Portuguese administration, and still sometime after Indian annexation, films in English, Hindi, or Marathi — which, together with Konkani, formed the range of Indian languages spoken in Goa — were subtitled in Portuguese. It was common that, on Sunday mornings, right after mass, English films were screened at the *Nacional*. Families would flock directly from church to the cinema, just in time for a film matinée. This mélange of religious practice and amusement was transversal to local life. The cinema gained such popularity that special screenings were organized during the Zatra, a Hindu festival which would see pilgrims rush to the Maruti temple, atop the Fontainhas district in Panjim. When the last session at the *Nacional* finally ended, not before 1 a.m., screenings would be held for the populace congregating from neighbouring villages, who would return home next morning, taking the first transport.

Any history of film in Portuguese India must credit the pioneering work of Antunes Amor. Amor was interviewed by magazine *Cinéfilo* apropos a screening of his film *Festa das Escolas de Nova Goa* [New Goa Schools Festival] at Lisbon's Central Cinema — the film was later screened as part of the Portuguese participation in the Antwerp Exposition. In this interview, he revealed that he had taken up cinematography inspired by the landscapes and 'exotic customs of Asians', in addition to the 'vestiges of the great Portuguese

[20] The *Nacional* was also a theatre, hosting several plays. The programme was circulated in the press and publicized by a car carrying a poster and someone who announced the titles through a megaphone. There was also a mobile 'hand', carrying the programme, which went around Panjim.
[21] Advertisements in *O Heraldo* indicate that, early in the month of November 1952, for example, from Friday to Monday, Orson Welles' *Macbeth* was screened, along with the Indian film *Sri Gurudev Datta*, which was programmed for the 'regular sessions'. November ended with the screening of *Jungle Headhunters*, an RKO production.

empire in the Orient'.[22]

Amor began filming in Macau and afterwards started to make amateur films in 'Portuguese India', presenting them at local cinemas. He announced he was planning a series of 'short documentaries, that will also show, for the first time amongst us, regional features of the State of India'.[23] Amor has several titles credited to him — *Vida Escolar em Nova Goa* [School Life in Nova Goa] (1930), *Goa: Índia Portuguesa* [Goa: Portuguese India] (1935), *Velha Cidade de Goa, Índia Portuguesa* [The Old City of Goa, Portuguese India] (1935), *Pelo Estado da Índia* [Travelling through the State of India] (1936), *Nos Lugares Indianos: Índia Portuguesa* [Visiting Indian Places: Portuguese India] (1936), *Curiosidades de Goa* [Jewels of Goa] (1937) — which are of dubious provenance. It is likely that Amor never directed this many films, but rather two or three that circulated with different titles, a common practice at the time, driven by the Law of 100 Metres.[24] The titles attributed to him seem disproportionate. Amor himself explains: 'Without State support and having had little time to film the aspects of India, I have few negatives of that colony of ours'.[25] Amor championed the cinematic projection of imperialism, understood the production process behind the documentaries about Africa, and blamed the administrators of eastern territories for the lack of propaganda films. He said:

> The cinematographic missions that went to Africa to make regional propaganda films, subsidized by their respective provincial governments, show Portugal the natural beauties, customs, agricultural production, industries, wealth and progress of our vast African possessions. [...] Only the Eastern colonies have failed to take advantage of regional films as a means of propaganda.[26]

It was so until the threat of annexation of Portuguese India by the Indian Union. If film production in Goa, local or Portuguese, had such little footing, would this have resulted, also, from high production costs and the distance from the metropolis? Would there have been local constraints that would have restricted production?

Contrary to British India, which had seen a rise in the number of active production companies with the arrival of sound film, Goa, Daman, and Diu suffered from a dearth of Portuguese production outlets and, starting in 1926, from the impositions ushered in by the dictatorship, which restricted individual liberties. If, until the 1930s, it was not surprising that there were

[22] R. S., 'Documentários das Nossas Colónias', *Cinéfilo*, 98 (1930), p. 8.
[23] Ibid.
[24] The '100 Metre Law' was passed in May 1927. Article no. 136 defined the obligation to exhibit, in every show, 'a film of Portuguese production at least 100 metres in length, containing Portuguese landscapes and of Portuguese screenplay and acting, which must be changed every week, and alternately screened as many times as possible'. This gave rise to a stratagem: the same film would circulate with different titles.
[25] R. S., 'Documentários das Nossas Colónias', *Cinéfilo*, 98 (1930), p. 8.
[26] Ibid.

almost no films made in Goa, then the situation contrasted with that of the other parts of India. Across non-Portuguese India, film production becomes increasingly widespread, resulting in the adoption of one of the most widely spoken languages, Hindi, as the vehicle that more generally can help avoid the multiplication of copies. In this context, and given the popularity of film in India, the production of propaganda in Portuguese was preceded by film production in Konkani, the local language. According to Andrew Greno Viegas, at least one documentary was shot as late as the 1940s, in Konkani, about the life of Christ, and screened at the *Swastik Cinema* and the *Old Pathé Cinema*, in Bombay, in 1948.[27]

Born in Mapusa, António Lawrence Jerry Braganza, who, when starting in film, adopted the artistic alias Al Jerry Braganza, moved to Bombay in 1940 to study at the Bombay Tutorial College. In *50 Years of Konkani Cinema* (2000), Viegas elucidates that Braganza held various positions in different production companies and that, aware of the profusion of films in English, Hindi, and Marathi, he wanted to make a Konkani film. The shooting started on 31 July 1949 and the film was finished nine months after, with six of these spent on filming. The government appears, in the meantime, to have introduced some restrictions on the production of films — not specified by Viegas. The film, since lost, was an adaptation of the Konkani novel *Mogachi Vodd*, by Dioguinho D'Mello, which told the love story between a wealthy man, played by the director, and a poor woman, played by Lena Fernandes. The screening of this feature was complemented by another, of a documentary about a procession in Goa carrying the image of Our Lady of Fátima, also directed by Braganza. The exterior shots included the filming of the Church of Velha Goa [Old Goa] and the Church of Mapusa, along with the Calangute Beach, the Mandovi River, the Forte Aguada, and the Altinho and Campal, all in Panjim. Together with the copy in Konkani, other versions of this film about religious commemorations and ceremonies, containing 'picturesque scenes' and views of Goa, were released in English, Hindi, and Portuguese.

Only in 1963 — after the annexation of Portuguese India — was the second Konkani fiction, *Amchem Noxib*, made. The most successful fictional film in Konkani, *Amchem Noxib* [Our Luck] was directed by A. Salam, with music and production by Frank Fernand. It starred Celestino Alvares and Rita Lobo. The film tells the misadventures of a Goan doctor, Dr Monteiro, from Panjim, who, on a work visit to Bombay, ends up in a nightclub, where he falls for Flavia, the resident singer. A professional concern drags him away from romantic idyll, but he instructs his assistant, Vales, to discover the singer's identity. In the meantime, Flavia's contract has ended, and she must return to Goa. Disconsolate, the doctor also goes back. And it is there that, after a few mishaps attuned to popular taste, the pair again meet.

---

[27] Andrew Greno Viegas, *50 years of Konkani Cinema* (Goa: Konkan Entertainment — Felizinha Viegas, 2000), p. 40.

According to what Shivendra Singh Dungarpur, from the Film Heritage Foundation, has stated to *The Indian Express*, on 8 February 2019, the long gap between the first and second films shot in Konkani must have resulted from the Portuguese government banning (sometime during the 1950s) the circulation of this type of film production.[28] On the other hand, Andrew Greno Viegas has claimed that 'during this period [between 1950 and 1963] some good Konkani films were abandoned halfway, like G. M. B. Rodrigues' *Sukhi Konn?*, C. Alvares' *Atancho Sounsar*, etc.' (*Goa Today*, June 2002).[29]

The success of the second Konkani fiction would have been a factor in Frank Fernand's not waiting that long to start his second production, *Nirmon* [Destiny] (1966). Featuring Shalini Mardolkar, Celestino Alvares, Anthony D'Sa, Jacint Vaz, Antonette Mendes, Ophelia, and Jack Souza Ferrao, this was a film inspired by the character in the homonymous poem by Tennyson Enoch Arden. The recipient of two Indian government awards presented by Indira Gandhi (Prime Minister at the time) — one to Celestino Alvares, for best actor — *Nirmon* was also celebrated for its soundtrack. The film was remade for Bollywood with the title *Taqdeer*, though the lead role was still played by Shalini Mardolkar, as in the original.

As for Al Jerry Braganza, he returned to Konkani films, in 1967, with *Sukhachem Sopon* [Dream of Bliss], the story of a love triangle, in which he also starred alongside the actresses Cecilia Machado and Antonette Mendes. Combining suspense, comedy and romantic about-faces, the film explores the dangers a young unwary Goan faces in Bombay. Ayres fancies Isabel, also from Goa, with whom he is engaged. However, the daughter of his boss in Bombay, Irene, is determined to get him to marry her.

These three Konkani fictions — *Sukhachem Sopon, Amchem Noxib* and *Nirmon* — are the only films still in the archives of the Department of Information and Publicity of the government of Goa. In the 1970s, the production of films in Konkani intensified and today a revaluation of the genre is starting to take place. Despite this, production remained residual, certainly because of difficulties during Portuguese control, but also because of the hegemony of Bollywood thereafter (as revealed by a certain post-annexation paucity), which imposed a specific mode of production and Hindi as the dominant language.

[28]   Not finding documentation about this ban, I wrote to Shivendra Singh Dungarpur asking for information on his source, but never received an answer. His statement can be found online at <https://indianexpress.com/article/entertainment/entertainment-others/now-showing-konkani-legacy/>.
[29]   Andrew Viegas, 'Konkani cinema', in *Updating News on the Tiatr Fraternity of Goa*, <https://tiatracademy.blogspot.com/2009_08_02_archive.html> [accessed 25 August 2024].

Cinema as Information and/or Propaganda in a Not So Portuguese Place

Official answers given to a UNESCO questionnaire 'about the means of information in Portugal and "overseas"' may not be thoroughly reliable, given how the collation process was managed.[30] However, they still reveal a few facts about the cinema phenomenon in the territories.

The questionnaire begins by asking general questions, about total land surface, population, main cities and resident population, proportion of urban versus country inhabitants, geographical segmentation of ethnic groups, spoken languages, geographical distribution of these languages and relative importance of each linguistic cluster, information about schools (including statistics on attendance), illiteracy numbers for each group, quality of life indicators before and after the war, and the state of electrification. Additionally, detailed questionnaires about film, the press and radio were also attached.

As far as 'Portuguese India' is concerned, the answers that remain (I could only find documentation relaying responses to the first 14 of around 40 questions) are synoptic. One learns that the Capital of Goa, Panjim, had 29,436 inhabitants, while the second city, Margao, had 17,933. The urban population was 12% of the total. The general population was characterized as being composed of 'whites, Luso-descendants, Indians, mestizos, yellows and blacks', specifying that 'whites' and 'Luso-descendants' were predominant in the capital and the main cities, and that the rest of the population was mainly Indian. Portuguese was, allegedly, the predominant language in the capital and urban areas. However, in the villages called The Old Conquests,[31] Konkani was the main language, with Marathi dominating in The New Conquests, and Gujarati in Daman and Diu. A remarkable fact about education was, already at that time, the profusion of English-speaking secondary schools: 65, attended by 13,477 students. These numbers were higher than those for primary students in Portuguese-speaking schools: 11,694, spread over 154 primary schools. As to the legislation and censorship laws that oversaw filmmaking activities, none existed that regulated the production and distribution of films. It is specified that a film censorship legislation project was being developed (which only came into effect in 1965, when it could no longer apply to Portuguese India), but

---

[30] The official document sent by the Ministry of Foreign Affairs to its Colonies counterpart, on 9 May 1951, states that it is not convenient that UNESCO 'approaches the Overseas Governments directly'. It considers that this contact must be mediated, such that a 'more effective control of the activity of that organism in Portuguese territory' is ensured. Earlier, on 25 April, Foreign Affairs had clarified that these enquiries suffered from 'a very special resentment, not really from the elements that they seek to collect but mainly because of the misuse that can intentionally be given to these'. It is written: 'there are many reasons to believe that such enquiries made in the so-called "dependent countries" will serve as a pretext for malicious criticisms which will target once more the colonial nations'. It is clarified that there is no drawback in answering the questions, but it is asserted that 'these answers will not be more than indications of legal dispositions and statistical or technical data, already published or known to all'.

[31] 'The Old Conquests' are a grouping of the areas in Goa which were incorporated into 'Portuguese India' early in the sixteenth century.

that, at the time, censorship, implemented by the Police Commissariat, obeyed government directives, which were, 'give or take', the same as those applied to the press. It is also clarified that there were no organizations for technicians, proprietors, or distributors. The number of cinemas or travelling cinemas is not given, but there were three thousand seats in theatres that could screen 35mm films. The programming, which changed twice a week, included newsreels, animation films, documentaries, and a feature film. There were 17 or 18 weekly sessions taking place in cinemas across the most important towns, but no theatres existed in rural areas. In 1950, total filmgoer numbers reached 284,118, and the average film ticket (which varied according to film genre and the status of the cinemas) cost a little over 146 rupees. Given the absence of Goan distributors, the films were provided by Indian and Portuguese distributors.

Political-Military Tension, Cultural Hybridity, and Catholicism in Late Propaganda

A survey of the local press reveals that more than a dozen cinemas operated until 1961 and that the films they screened were mostly of Indian and Hollywood production. Bizarrely, or maybe not, when it comes to Portuguese fiction, only one article can be found, about the screening, on 25 November 1951, of the feature film *Camões: Erros Meus, Má Fortuna, Amor Ardente* [Camões: My Errors, Cruel Fortune, Ardent Love] (Leitão de Barros, 1946), about the life of the eponymous poet, who, in the poem *Os Lusíadas* [The Lusiads], eulogized Vasco da Gama's trip to India. Even though the film was endorsed by Ferro and considered to be of national interest by a Salazar decree — in 1946, the Secretariat had presented it with several awards — it could never be claimed to be to popular taste. Camões's journey through Goa, added to his association with the discovery of the sea route to India by Vasco da Gama, would have been a factor in the choosing of a film which, when screened in Panjim, was already several years old.

In the mid-1950s, probably because of the protests by the satyagrahis at the border, which resulted in the assassination of two dozen protesters by the Portuguese army, several propaganda newsreel editions, called *Imagens de Portugal* [Images of Portugal], sponsored by the SNI, began to be screened in various Goan cinemas. In an article in *O Heraldo*, from 17 January 2021, Cristo Prazeres da Costa[32] mentions that, as a consequence of the growing anti-colonialist sentiment in Goa, the Portuguese authorities resorted to the mobilization of the army, and the 'Lusitanização' [*Lusitanization*] of places, programming the free screening of Portuguese films in the central squares of the three main Goan cities.[33] *Amor de Perdição* [Doomed Love] (António Lopes Ribeiro, 1943) — whose protagonist, Simão, is condemned to exile in Goa for

[32] Son of the late Amadeu Prazeres da Costa, former chief editor of *O Heraldo*.
[33] <https://www.heraldgoa.in/Review/Cinema-e-recreio-dos-anos-50-em-Goa/169851>.

committing a crime of passion — *Frei Luís de Sousa* (António Lopes Ribeiro, 1950), *As Pupilas do Sr. Reitor* [The Rector's Pupils] (Leitão de Barros, 1935), *Um Homem do Ribatejo* [A Man from Ribatejo] (Henrique Campos, 1946), and *A Morgadinha dos Canaviais* [The Heiress to the Cane Fields] (Caetano Bonucci, 1949) are the films that were shown. Note that these are all quite old, in black and white, and fit well within the choice to provide an accessible adaptation of classic Portuguese literature.

The first propaganda documentaries about Portuguese India did not predate the screening of fictional films from Portugal by much. The 24 October 1952 edition of the Goan newspaper *Diário da Noite* reports that Ricardo Malheiro had made a film in Macau, after a stopover in Portuguese India. The account is flattering, portraying Malheiro as a 'prestigious producer, a dynamic and competent director'. Malheiro had the support of an operator but, according to the *Diário da Noite*, his success was 'solely down to his dynamism, his intelligence and workmanship, and his profound knowledge of the cinema'. The article also alludes to *Caminhos de S. Francisco Xavier* [Saint Francis Xavier's Ways]:

> It is once again a most opportune film, which Ricardo Malheiro's vision unveiled from afar, for it is this year that we celebrate the fourth centenary since the death of the greatest missionary of all ages, and nothing better than a film to make him even better known, the Great Saint, and show the places where so many souls were converted by him to Christ's religion, opening the way to the missionaries who, across all the Orient, spread the word of God and the name of Portugal.[34]

During his trip to Goa, Malheiro also directed *Roteiro do Mandovi: Velha Goa* [Mandovani Guide: Old Goa] and *A Viagem de Sua Excelência o Ministro do Ultramar ao Oriente 1: Índia* [His Excellency the Overseas Minister's Trip to the Orient 1: India]. A survey of the local papers indicates that he filmed in 1951 but did not return in 1952 for the commemorations devoted to Saint Francis Xavier.[35] However, he is credited with the authorship of the documentary *A Exposição Colonial em Goa* [The Colonial Exposition in Goa] (1953), which was organized in parallel.

Several political-military incidents are registered in *Operação de Segurança no Estado da Índia* [Security Operation in the State of India] (1955), author unknown and soundtrack lost, deposited at the Centro de Audiovisuais do Exército [Army Audio-visual Centre] (CAVE). The film propagandizes the dictatorship's version of the incidents with the satyagrahis near the border with Goa, which, in 1955, amplified the continuing tension with the Indian government. At CAVE, there is also the film *Rumo à Índia* [Towards India] (1959, soundtrack lost), directed by Miguel Spiguel, about the sending of troops to the territory. Together with his military films, the documentaries directed

---

[34]   N/a, *Diário da Noite*, 24 October 1952, p. 1.
[35]   The local press identifies the reporters present in Goa but never refers to Malheiro.

by Spiguel for the AGU include *Aguarelas da Índia Portuguesa* [Watercolours of Portuguese India] (1959), *Dança do Mandó e Paisagem Goesa* [Mando Dance and Goan Landscape] (1960, soundtrack lost, incomplete print), archived at the Portuguese Cinematheque, along with *Manhã de Sol em Damão* [Sunny Morning in Daman] (1959) and *Romagem a Diu* [Heading to Diu] (1959), which have records at CAVE, but remain inaccessible. These are all propaganda films which underline local exoticism through narration, while in the images they exhibit the socio-cultural specificities forged by the encounter between the Portuguese and the Indian, shown in religious, architectural, and cultural notes.

To close this cycle, one can also consider *Honra à Índia Portuguesa* [Honour to Portuguese India] (1961), no. 239 in the newsreel series *Imagens de Portugal*, evocative of the history of the Portuguese presence in India. The film asserts the illegality of the annexation of Goa, Daman, and Diu by the Indian Union, carried out despite the Hague International Criminal Court's recognition of Portuguese rights over those territories.

This official filmography, assembled quite late, displays the existing tensions — in the records detailing the transfer of troops and the conflicts with the satyagrahis — and, mainly through the voiceover, by questioning the pacifism of the Indian government, accusing it of transgressions, concealing the fact that, since the nineteenth century, local revolts against Portuguese rule already existed, later intensified by the loss of freedom that arrived with the dictatorship.

Conclusion

Despite the stratification of the colonies performed by the dictatorship, upheld without questioning as regards the political rhetoric sustaining the imposed social hierarchization, there persists a tendency to investigate the 'Portuguese Orient' without analysing the specificities of the discourse about each territory or the particularities of the identities of the (schematically) represented communities — a fact that extends, also, to the research about the former African colonies.

The characterization made by the regime rested on the propagation of a mythology affirming multiculturalism and the acceptance of diverse cults, despite the proclaimed Christian evangelist nature of the colonial project. This evangelism was effectively downplayed, as far as the Orient was concerned, by a characterization which integrated distinct representations of the local peoples of each territory. In the process of social and racial stratification enforced by the regime, the older and more elaborate a culture appeared to be, the higher its placing in the colonial pyramid — such as with the inhabitants of 'Portuguese

India'.[36] When we consider the voiceover, however, the film archive blurs — almost reverses — the cultural specificities which the images, often chosen for their exoticism, show. In the voiceover there reverberates the discourse about the inherent difference in Portuguese colonialism, which, starting in the 1950s, becomes Luso-tropicalism orientalized, that is, Luso-orientalism.

This Luso-orientalism tries to impose the idea that the 'Portuguese Orient' is a Lusitanian creation — and this rhetoric is transversal to the narration in film productions. Every filmed projection, regardless of differences between each territory that comprises the 'Orient', or between these and the African lands, affirms, through the voiceover, the exemplarity of Portuguese colonialization — always contested by the other European empires.

In Portuguese propaganda films, 'Portuguese India' is shown as an example for its reception of Christianity, and for being the place where the 'Portuguese way of being in the world' started to materialize. However, despite this propagandistic 'projection', Hinduism remained dominant, and Portuguese was only spoken by a minority. The struggle for independence was already in progress in the nineteenth century. After the fall of the First Portuguese Republic, when the limits to civil rights imposed by the dictatorship amplified discontentment, the local desire for autonomy was suppressed by the regime's growing brutality. Until 1961, the tension around the demands for administrative independence and the respect for civil rights never stopped growing. And in a society stratified by castes, those rights were a demand of the privileged. Regarding film, the effort by local professionals to build a Konkani production faced a lack of support from the Portuguese administration — which, according to Amor, failed to back even the propaganda films. This type of production only received backing much later, from the AGU — absorbed into the hegemony of a production model centred on Bollywood, which privileged the Hindi language and Hindu culture.

When the diplomatic channels collapsed — after the Portuguese assault on the satyagrahis as they peacefully entered the territory — propaganda films became an important exhibition and production tool. A survey of the themes that were filmed suggests an exaltation of the Christian framework employed by the Portuguese administration and the importance of religion. This exaltation also articulates the dissemination of the rhetoric about the supposed 'Portuguese way of being in the world' — including details about the multiplicity of cults, landscapes, and cultural practices — with an apparent valorization of miscegenation, which, in the official discourse, is potentiated by the meeting and synthesis of Portuguese and oriental cultures.

This late venturing into propaganda films about Portuguese India, to be

---

[36] This is a similar process to that which also propelled the Cape Verdeans and Santomeans to a higher ranking. However, whereas in Portuguese India it pertained mostly to a perception of long history and sophistication, in the case of Cape Verde and São Tomé it was a direct product of far greater assimilation (forcible or otherwise).

shown in the metropolis, or the attempt to 'make-India-more-Lusitanian' carried out by the Portuguese, through the screening of films still made under the aegis of Ferro's 'Política do espírito [spiritual policy] — a cinema of literary adaptations and historical figures — succeeded, however, only residually and had little impact, at a time when the loss of Portuguese India already looked inevitable (as residual as the Portuguese presence already was, also in terms of military numbers, it dropped further with the start of the war of liberation in Angola). Today, these films remain valuable as a 'symptom' of the perception the regime had of the situation and of the discourse it wanted to project, which had little actual effect.

A Transcivilizational Island:
A Ilha dos Amores, by Paulo Rocha

PAULO CUNHA

Universidade da Beira Interior

'bring together all cultures, all arts, all styles, all languages'
— PAULO ROCHA

Directed by the Portuguese Paulo Rocha, and premiered at the Cannes Film Festival in 1982, *A Ilha dos Amores* is a film about the relationship between West and East as seen through the eyes of Portuguese poet and diplomat Wenceslau de Moraes, who was born in Lisbon (1854), and lived in Macau (1891–98) and in Japan (1898–1929), where he died. The film is also marked by the work of the Chinese poet Chu Yuan (343 BC–278 BC) and the Portuguese poet Luís Vaz de Camões (1524–1580), in an intersection of literary and cultural universes that makes this a transcivilizational narrative.

This paper demonstrates how *A Ilha dos Amores* remains a transcivilizational filmic space, essentially because it breaks any exclusive logic (which serves to exclude) of nationality or national culture, broadening its horizon in an approach outside a defined time or space. Paulo Rocha summons multiple narrative references from different materialities to build a utopia, a comprehensive dialogue between civilizations (as set of values and practices common to certain territories) with different cosmovisions. The aim is to highlight and understand these relationships, from literature to theatre and other arts, and reflect on the mediating role of cinema in evoking and reframing the past.

Rocha and Japan

Paulo Rocha was born in 1935, in Porto, on the western tip of the European continent, the son of an emigrant family that had made a fortune in Brazil, even further to the west. However, among other aesthetic influences, Japan began to have a prominent place very early in his life. In 1955, still far from thinking about a film career, Rocha was very impressed with *Jigokumon [Gate of Hell]* (1953),[1] a historical drama directed by Teinosuke Kinugasa about a samurai who tries to marry an escort lady-in-waiting he has saved, discovering later that she is already married. *Gate of Hell* won the grand prize award at the 1954 Cannes

---

[1] Paulo Rocha, 'O Diário das Ilhas', in *Paulo Rocha: O Rio do Ouro* (Lisbon: Cinemateca Portuguesa, 1996), p. 36.

Portuguese Studies vol. 40 no. 2 (2024), doi:10.1353/port.00013, pp. 159–74

Film Festival, an Academy Honorary Award for 'Best Foreign Language Film first released in the United States during 1954', and the Golden Leopard at the Locarno International Film Festival.

In 1996, in response to an invitation from the Cinemateca Portuguesa, Rocha chose eleven films by other directors to accompany a full retrospective cycle that the Cinemateca dedicated to him that year. Of the eleven choices, one was Portuguese, one Italian, two from the US, three French and four were Japanese films — *Naniwa reji* (1936, Mizoguchi), *Jujiro* (1928, Kinugasa), *Khoyagawa-ke no Aki* (1961, Ozu) and *Nippon Sengoshi* (1970, Imamura) — which seems to reveal the influence of Japanese cinema on his formation and film culture.

Actress Isabel Ruth recalls that Paulo Rocha used to tell a lot of stories about Japan during breaks in the filming of the film *Mudar de Vida*, shot in Portugal between October and December 1965. But Rocha's first trip to Japan would only take place the following year, in 1966, travelling in the company of Takano Etsuko, a friend that he had met in Paris, at the film school (IDHEC) that they both attended. The purpose of the visit was to start a film project about the history of the introduction of firearms into Japan by the Portuguese (1542), based on an episode reported in the *Peregrinação* (published posthumously in 1614), by Fernão Mendes Pinto (1511–1583), a Portuguese writer and adventurer who sailed the Asian coast for several years (1553–67), including China and Japan. In 1967, a further trip to Japan took Paulo Rocha to the south of the territory, to Tokushima, where he got to know the life and work of the Portuguese-born poet Wenceslau de Moraes, who had fled Portugal at the end of the nineteenth century to seek in Japan an 'art of living' that reconciled the material and the spiritual.[2] Finally, in 1979 Rocha moved to Japan where he would work until 1983 as a cultural attaché at the Portuguese embassy in Tokyo. It was during this phase that Rocha shot two lengthy tribute-studies of the life of Wenceslau de Moraes, *A Ilha dos Amores* (1982) and *A Ilha de Moraes* (1984).

A Ilha dos Amores takes a poetic and performative look at the life of Wenceslau de Moraes, a Portuguese writer, military officer and diplomat who was born in Lisbon (1854), lived in Mozambique and Macau, and died in Japan (1929). Moraes's love life and marriage also make up the plot of the film: his mistress in Lisbon, his Chinese family in Macau, his second Japanese wife and her niece. While his literary work is recognized in Portugal, Moraes ends his life in Kobe, with his kimono in tatters, his beard overgrown, lonely, becoming a kind of ghost, lost in contemplation of nature, who wanders at night around the graves of his last loves. Death comes in unclear circumstances: is it suicide, murder, accident?

In 1972, with financial support from the Calouste Gulbenkian Foundation, the filmmakers' cooperative Centro Português de Cinema (CPC) awarded production support to the project *A Ilha dos Amores*. However, due to production difficulties, Rocha would relinquish the subsidy, which would be

---

[2]   Synopsis of DVD Paulo Rocha Vol. 3.

transferred to two medium-length projects: *Jaime* (1974, António Reis) and *Fragmentos de um Filme-Esmola* (1973, João César Monteiro). In 1973, *A Ilha dos Amores* would appear again in the CPC's production plan. In March 1974, the Instituto Português de Cinema (IPC) awarded a subsidy of around US$370,000 (1974 values) to support the production of *A Ilha dos Amores*.[3] However, the CPC and IPC production plans would suffer several delays due to the Carnation Revolution, which began in April 1974. The production of *A Ilha dos Amores* would begin in 1978, with the shooting of the 'Portuguese part' of the film in Lisbon, namely at the Tobis film studios, in the Largo do Rossio, at the Military Museum and at the Navy Museum. This first phase of production lasted 90 days of shooting. In addition to three days of filming in Macau, the shooting in Japan lasted another eighteen days, always from 9 a.m. to 6 p.m., after about four months of preparation.[4] During this period, the director also finished shooting *A Ilha de Moraes* (1984), a documentary about the life of Wenceslau de Moraes.

In short, for the shooting and editing alone, Rocha devoted around five years to the project (1978–82), but the filmmaker dedicated himself to this project in an unprecedented way: 'There was a language problem, not only with the Japanese language, which I studied for twenty years until I was able to use it professionally in filming and writing, as well as trying to adapt myself to the closed world, full of small rules in human relations, and in artistic creativity, which govern traditional Japanese arts.'[5]

The first version of what would become the script for *A Ilha dos Amores* was written over the course of a few years, having been completed in Japan, between 1969 and 1970.[6] As Rocha admits, the first draft of *A Ilha dos Amores* proceeded from the production of his short film *A Pousada das Chagas* (1972), providing the filmmaker with an opportunity to experiment with a new creative method, based on the collage process. In this he was inspired by the German composer Karlheinz Stockhausen, saying: 'collage comes to dominate my work. [...] The shape of *A Ilha dos Amores* came from *A Pousada das Chagas*. [...] The collage work inside and outside the sequence shot, which started there, reaches a formal maturity in *A Ilha dos Amores*.'[7] From this idea of collage, *A Ilha dos Amores* emerges with a kaleidoscopic mosaic of countless cultural and artistic references which are examined in detail in the following sections.

---

[3] For comparative reference, *Daisy Miller* (1974, Peter Bogdanovich) had a budget of 2.2 million dollars and *La Nuit américaine/Day for Night* (1973, François Truffaut) had a budget of 700,000 dollars.
[4] Rocha, *Rio do Ouro*, p. 84.
[5] Rocha, *Rio do Ouro*, p. 83.
[6] Rocha, *Rio do Ouro*, p. 81.
[7] Rocha, *Rio do Ouro*, p. 80.

Literature

Rocha's contact with the work *The Nine Songs*, an anthology of poems attributed to the Chinese politician and poet Qu Yuan (*c.* 340 BC–278 BC), 'provided the solution to the problem of form and background', but also 'integrated the Macau of Camões' cave, Pessanha, Moraes (and Patrício, who died there years later) into the film as a whole.' Finally, Qu Yuan's poems would help to balance Portuguese 'sentimentality' with the 'tension' that Rocha had envisioned for *A Ilha dos Amores*, nipping 'sensitive tenderness in the bud'.[8]

According to Rocha,[9] Qu Yuan is 'one of the great founding heroes of the Chinese identity', mainly due to his supposedly patriotic suicide, which made him a kind of 'romantic hero who has periodically been claimed by Chinese intellectuals seeking to escape the classicism and the rationalism of the Confucian tradition'. Over the centuries, Qu Yuan also became, in popular tradition, a reference throughout the Far East, 'from Korea to Japan and China', with a great annual feast: 'on the night of his death, to appease his spirit, people go to the rivers and throw offerings onto lighted boats that float along the flowing waters (as seen in the movie *Lord Jim*). The "Dragon Boat" regattas, from Singapore to Nagasaki, via Macau, are part of the same tradition.'

Another reference work for this film was *Os Lusíadas* (1572), an epic poem in ten cantos written by Luís Vaz de Camões (1524–1580). The title of Rocha's film is adopted from the myth that Camões recounts in Cantos IX and X of *Os Lusíadas*: led by Venus, the Portuguese navigators arrive at an idyllic island inhabited by nymphs who engage in erotic and amorous games with the navigators; the Nymph Tétis offers a feast to Vasco da Gama and his navigators, later taking him to discover the 'machine of the world'; the navigators return to Lisbon, accompanied by the Nymphs.

Even though the episode became known as 'A Ilha dos Amores', Vítor Aguiar e Silva points out that such an expression never appears in the Camonian poem, where it is called the 'ínsula divina' [divine isle] (*Os Lusíadas*, IX, 21), 'Ilha namorada' [beloved island] (IX, 51), 'Ilha ... fresca e bela' [fresh and beautiful island] (IX, 52), 'fermosa Ilha, alegre e deleitosa' [beautiful island, joyful and delightful] (IX, 54), 'Ilha angélica pintada' [painted angelic island] (IX, 89), 'Ilha de Vénus' [island of Venus] (IX, 95) and 'Ilha alegre e namorada' [happy and beloved island] (X, 143).[10] Although fictional, this literary island has been associated by several authors with real islands: Santa Helena (in the South Atlantic), Terceira (Azores, North Atlantic), Cape Verde (North Atlantic), Madeira (North Atlantic), Canary Islands (North Atlantic), Angediva (in the Arabian Sea, south of Goa), Zanzibar (South Indian Ocean), Ceylon (now Sri Lanka, North Indian Ocean) or Bombay (India, North Indian Ocean). However,

---

[8]   Rocha, *Rio do Ouro*, p. 81.
[9]   Rocha, *Rio do Ouro*, p. 82.
[10]   Vítor Aguiar e Silva, 'Ilha dos Amores (Episódio da)', in *Dicionário de Luís de Camões* (Lisbon: Caminho, 2012), pp. 437–44 (p. 437).

Silva argues that, 'without prejudice to Camões having used memories of a concrete island, the "Ilha dos Amores" is an imagined and imaginary island, a symbolic island that, as such, cannot be identified with an empirical referent'.[11]

However, there is still a debate about whether this symbolic island is to be found in the Atlantic or in the Indian Ocean, but Silva does not hesitate to state that the 'island of Venus is an island that the goddess displaced from the eastern Mediterranean to the Indian waters', with a description marked by Camões's 'intertextual memories' coming from 'Greco-Latin poetry and Renaissance Italian poetry'.[12] Was it this classical affiliation, for example, that justified the collage by Rocha of an adaptation of the beginning of the work *De Rerum Natura*, a didactic poem written in the first century BC by Lucretius, in the episode of Invocation to Venus (shots 15 to 19) of the film *A Ilha dos Amores*?

I conclude, therefore, that the process of idealizing Camões's Island resulted from the fusion of different intertextual, transgeographical and trans-chronological matrices. In addition to these matrices, Camões's own personal path is relevant: 'he dominates a vast culture', including authors such as Virgil (70–19 BC), Ovid (43 BC–18 AD), Horace (65–8 BC) and Homer (eighth century BC), and others he knows indirectly through the 'consultation of erudite manuals', anthologies, encyclopedias and grammar books. Of his personal trajectory, we know that he began his military career in Ceuta, in North Africa, where 'he was wounded in one eye'; in 1553 he left for India, settling in Goa, from where he travelled on expeditions to the Straits of Mecca and the Persian Gulf; he then travelled to Macau, ending up shipwrecked at the mouth of the Mekong River, in the south of present-day Vietnam; and after living in Mozambique for two years he finally returned to Portugal, in 1570.[13]

Helena Buescu proposes a reading hypothesis for the Camonian Island of Love 'as a figurative invention of an imaginary utopian reality'.[14] Although it does not follow the model of Thomas More ('an ideal and socially organized city, which regulates social behaviour from the political, moral and sexual points of view'), the 'Ilha dos Amores' 'offers a set of utopian characteristics', namely 'the allegorical and symbolic sense', the erotic element.[15] In short, Buescu considers that 'the recovery of *nostos* underlines the fact that the Ilha dos Amores is more a utopia-as-impulse than a program'.[16] Buescu interprets this episode in a very particular way, as the 'origin of a new human race', which 'will materialize in a time and place to come: Portugal'.[17]

---

[11] Silva, 'Ilha dos Amores (Episódio da)', p. 438.
[12] Silva, 'Ilha dos Amores (Episódio da)', p. 438.
[13] Maria Vitalina Leal de Matos, 'Biografia de Luís Vaz de Camões', in *Dicionário de Luís de Camões* (Lisbon: Caminho, 2012), pp. 80–94.
[14] Helena Buescu, 'Utopia e História: *Os Lusíadas* (Camões) e *Uma viagem à Índia* (Gonçalo Tavares)', in *Poesia Contemporânea e Tradição: Brasil — Portugal* (São Paulo: Nankin Editorial, 2017), pp. 127–40 (p. 128).
[15] Buescu, 'Utopia e História', p. 129.
[16] Buescu, 'Utopia e História', p. 130.
[17] Buescu, 'Utopia e História', p. 135.

For Pedro Fonseca, who analyses the vision of the cultural and geographical landscape of the Orient visited by Camões's epic vision, *Os Lusíadas* is 'a work committed to traces of the ethno-cultural-androcentric complex characteristic of the western tradition', being an example of an 'imposition of the masculine (West) over the feminine (East) in a cultural and geographical perspective'.[18] He also demonstrates that 'the patriarchal always ends up being associated with the epic and virility in legitimizing the West's dominance over the Eastern periphery, usually equated with prejudiced attributes to identify the nature of the feminine'.[19] The Cantos of Camões's epic dedicated to 'Ilha dos Amores', in particular, 'constitute the metaphor of the Orient identified with the erotic and sexual'.[20] They are also clear examples of an association of the conquest idea with erotic-sexual images, projecting a 'desiring expectation of the Westerner' in relation to an Eastern space 'tendentially feminized', sensualized and discriminated against as 'a passive receptivity':

> This search for a central point as a locus of historical and cultural reason and morals (SHOHAT, 1994, p. 141), inherent to the Lusitanity heroicized by Camões, irrationalizes and demoralizes the peripheral eastern regions, which are now projected as places of impulses, violent instincts and anarchic lust (SHOHAT, 1994, p. 141), demanding the control and domination of the European conqueror.[21]

In short, according to Fonseca, 'this trope of the unbridled amorous licentiousness of the East represents, in Camonian discourse, one of the strategic aspects of the Eurocentrism of the time, committed to the cultural and moral subalternization of the other in reference to the East.'[22] Camões's 'Ilha dos Amores' promotes a hierarchical narrative among the nymphs who appear as 'obedient and gentle trophies of erotic refreshment' that will reward the 'honourable performance of the virile and epic Portuguese in the conquest of the sea route to the Indies'.[23] Finally, the 'mythical and luxurious oceanic island functions as a true *locus amoenus* which, reminiscent of the golden tradition of classical antiquity, adds to it the empire of pleasure and sensuality'.[24]

After the Cantos by Qu Yuan and Camões, *The Cantos*, by the American poet Ezra Pound (1885–1972), is another reference assumed by Paulo Rocha.[25] An epic poem divided into 120 sections, written between 1915 and 1962, *The Cantos* is Pound's life's work, a true map for the evolution of his literary creation, reflecting all his erudition and itinerancy (he was born in the state

---

[18]   Pedro Carlos Louzada Fonseca, 'O Oriente de *Os Lusíadas* de Camões: representação épica e discurso de Gênero', *Polifonia*, 16 (2008), 59–70 (p. 59).
[19]   Fonseca, 'O Oriente de *Os Lusíadas* de Camões...', p. 60.
[20]   Fonseca, 'O Oriente de *Os Lusíadas* de Camões...', p. 65.
[21]   Fonseca, 'O Oriente de *Os Lusíadas* de Camões...', p. 63; Ella Shohat and Robert Stam, *Unthinking Eurocentrism: Multiculturalism and the Media* (London and New York: Routledge, 1994).
[22]   Fonseca, 'O Oriente de *Os Lusíadas* de Camões...', p. 65.
[23]   Fonseca, 'O Oriente de *Os Lusíadas* de Camões...', p. 67.
[24]   Fonseca, 'O Oriente de *Os Lusíadas* de Camões...', p. 67.
[25]   Rocha, *Rio do Ouro*, p. 81.

of Idaho and grew up in New York, but lived parts of his adult life in England, France and Italy) and revealing all his process of recreating the traditions with which he came into contact.[26]

In addition to the modern character of his writing, and his intervention, Pound's attraction to Chinese writing (the ideogram) and culture and to Japanese theatre[27] was another relevant element in common with Rocha, as well as the multiplicity and intersection of references contained in his writing: 'From the classical world of Greece to Renaissance Italy, from China in the T'sung dynasty to America during and after the War of Independence, the poem contains an encyclopedic range of allusion and reference.'[28] Rocha even confesses a particular fascination with Pound and his mania for 'bringing together all cultures, all arts, all styles, all languages'.[29] A good example of this desire is the initial scene filmed in Japan, on the terrace of the Wako house, in which the actors summon the spirits of the characters they will play: 'There was a mixture of languages: each one spoke his own, in a chain of words in Japanese and Portuguese.' The text of this scene results from a 'collage' 'of certain Noh plays: Matsukaze, Atsumori, etc.' with 'a Chinese poem translated by Pessanha, and poems by Camões'.[30]

Another literary presence is Luiza Neto Jorge (1939–1989), a Portuguese poet and translator, who translated Apollinaire, Aragon, Breton, Nerval, Genet, Yourcenar, Artaud, Céline, Éluard, Ionesco, Michaux, Raimond Queneau, Jarry, and Vian. Trained in Romanic Philology, she lived in Paris between 1962 and 1970. Influenced by the surrealist legacy and by its ability to dialogue with the lyrical tradition, she was also the author of film scripts (for Alberto Seixas Santos, Solveig Nordlund, Jorge Silva Melo, and Margarida Gil) and theatrical adaptations (of Diderot).[31] Responsible for the dialogues of A Ilha dos Amores, Luiza Neto Jorge was, in the words of Rocha, a writer with 'irony', 'courage' and 'intelligence you could cut with a knife', along with an extreme disregard for sentimentality, 'Anti-idealist, anti... anti-everything that we were, boys of our time who came to tempt her with scenes and with movies'. The poet spent 'years working on the texts, in a relentless effort. When she finally delivered them, they were imperious, sublime, definitive dialogues.'[32]

With so many and such diverse references, Luiza Neto Jorge's work involved 'putting together, according to the logic of modern poetry, fragments upon fragments [...], the ironies, the ruptures, the jumps were huge but they were in line with the content of the scene.'[33] With half of the dialogues spoken

[26] Ira B. Nadel (ed.), The Cambridge Companion to Ezra Pound (Cambridge: Cambridge University Press, 1999), p. 1.
[27] Nadel, The Cambridge Companion to Ezra Pound, pp. 1–2.
[28] Nadel, The Cambridge Companion to Ezra Pound, p. 4.
[29] Rocha, Rio do Ouro, p. 81.
[30] Rocha, Rio do Ouro, p. 91.
[31] Gastão Cruz, A poesia portuguesa hoje (Lisbon: Relógio d'Água, 1999), pp. 153–63.
[32] Rocha, Rio do Ouro, p. 27.
[33] Rocha, Rio do Ouro, p. 92.

in Japanese, there was also a Japanese screenwriter (Sumiko Haneda, an experienced documentary filmmaker in the post-World War II era), who adapted them after a translation from Portuguese into Japanese done by Paulo Rocha himself. Due to the pressure of time and the volume of work in pre-production and during shooting, Rocha confesses that he did not understand, at the time, all the complexity of Luiza Neto Jorge's texts: 'Years later, when I had to spend months translating the dialogues into Japanese and French, I realized, "too late", the infinity of paths that the texts proposed and that we hadn't had time to explore'.[34]

According to Rocha, the Portuguese poet Cesário Verde (1855–1886) and his poem *O Sentimento dum Ocidental* [*The Feeling of a Westerner*], included in *O Livro de Cesário Verde* (1887), are also present in *A Ilha dos Amores*, namely as a reference to the 'tired air by the weight of urban life' that Rocha recognized in the bodies of inhabitants of the most central and popular neighbourhoods of Tokyo at dusk.[35] In these same passages, the colourful neons of the Tokyo landscape refer the viewer to 'the old gods of Greece and Rome, more powerful than ever, who are in our unconscious': 'Venus is celebrated every day on Kodak propaganda posters, and Revlon. The figuration is the same, revised by the Renaissance. The positions, attitudes, bodies are the same.'[36]

The *niki*, Japanese intimate diaries from the thirteenth and fourteenth centuries — with which, according to Rocha, 'there is nothing to compare to in Western literature' — are also texts of 'great modernity', whose collages of 'micro-units' and 'fragments' are also very much present in *A Ilha dos Amores*.[37]

The scene set in Macau, from shots 43 to 47, also required a scenographic work that sought to synthesize this West–East dialogue: 'For this sequence I read a lot of Chinese and English sources about the last hundred years of "foreign" cities on the seas, from China — Shanghai and Hong Kong mainly — and I asked a lot of people in Macau.'[38]

Theatre

A Ilha dos Amores only came to fruition due to the close collaboration with the Teatro da Cornucópia. Founded in 1973, the company promoted 'a work in which classical roots and current experimentation merged', something that particularly pleased Paulo Rocha: 'I accompanied the adventure of discovering the individual poetics of Jorge and Luís Miguel through the theatre repertoire, from Roman times to present-day Germany.'[39] The collaborative creative process with Cornucópia, which took a long time, also suffered strong external

[34] Rocha, *Rio do Ouro*, p. 27.
[35] Rocha, *Rio do Ouro*, p. 93.
[36] Rocha, *Rio do Ouro*, pp. 93–94.
[37] Rocha, *Rio do Ouro*, pp. 101–02.
[38] Rocha, *Rio do Ouro*, p. 97.
[39] Rocha, *Rio do Ouro*, p. 83.

influences: 'we talked about the echo and rhythm of the actors' steps in certain scenes and about the construction of the respective decors, the wooden stairs, the floor resonating like a drum, in the style of Noh theatre, the notes to be inserted in the intervals of the steps and voices of the actors, as in Kabuki theatre.'[40]

In addition to Luís Miguel Cintra (playing Wenceslau de Moraes) and Jorge Silva Melo (playing the 'painter'), scenographer Cristina Reis and musician Paulo Brandão also collaborated actively in *A Ilha dos Amores*. Zita Duarte (who played Francisca) and Maria Paola Porru (sound director in the film) were also occasional contributors to Cornucópia. In Canto IX, the scene 'Os Mistérios do Real' (shots 113 to 115) is particularly 'indebted to the poetics of the "realism" of the Cornucopia, a realism with Germanic roots, which went through the experiences of Berlin modernism'.[41]

But the film was also heavily influenced by traditional Japanese theatre, in particular Noh theatre, which stood out especially in the Muromachi period (1333–1573), Japan's medieval era. With popular origins, due to the protection and financial promotion of shogun Yoshimitsu Ashikaga, the Noh theatre gradually transforms itself into a more elitist and ritualistic show, also inserting itself into a religious pedagogical context, with theatre companies linked to a large temple or shrine, in which Noh seeks to teach viewers 'the path of soul salvation'.[42]

Known as a 'theatre of masks', Noh theatre proposes an interaction between spirits (the *shite*, protagonist, and his companion) and living people (*waki*, supporting actor, and his companion), seeking to express themselves with a minimum of language or movements.[43] One of the opening rituals of the film *A Ilha dos Amores*, with the Tokyo landscape in the background, in which the actors in the film summon the spirits of the dead to return and reincarnate in their bodies, reflects the influence of Noh theatre: 'This call of the spirits of the dead for the actors connects Noh theatre (which dates back to the fourteenth century and is Japanese) to its remote origins, to the ancient ceremonies of the Nine Songs in China. In both, it was a question of, ritually, through dance, bringing the spirits back to earth.'[44]

The stage of the Noh theatre was built from Japanese cypress, with great architectural care, highlighting the stage that advances towards the audience, 'which surrounds you and watches the show in a solemn attitude', as in Shakespearean theatre.[45] For example, the bath scene in *A Ilha dos Amores* (shot 52) is very marked by this scenic reference: 'The bamboos come from the stages of the Noh theatre. From Noh also comes the outside balcony through

[40]   Rocha, *Rio do Ouro*, p. 83.
[41]   Rocha, *Rio do Ouro*, p. 112.
[42]   Darci Kusano, *Teatro Tradicional Japonês* (São Paulo: Fundação Japão, 2013), p. 5.
[43]   Kusano, *Teatro Tradicional Japonês*, p. 6.
[44]   Rocha, *Rio do Ouro*, p. 91.
[45]   Kusano, *Teatro Tradicional Japonês*, p. 6.

which Isabel advances: it is the *hashigakari*, through which the actors enter.'[46]
In this particular scene, 'the ending comes from Japanese puppetry, *bunraku*,
where the operator, in full view of the audience, manipulates the larger puppets.
[...] In puppet theatre, characters sometimes talk about themselves as if they
were other people.'[47] The influence of the Noh theatre can also be seen in
terms of sound: 'the decor itself is a giant musical instrument', because under
the wooden floor of the stage there are clay vessels where the actor can make
sounds like a drum.[48]

Another traditional Japanese theatrical form present in the work of Paulo
Rocha is the Kabuki theatre, which developed mainly in the Edo period (1603–
1867), the Japanese feudal era, in which the country's international isolation
allowed Japanese culture to experience a period of great flowering, from
painting to literature, passing through the theatre. In a phase dominated by
Confucian philosophy, society experienced 'clashes between social duties and
moral obligations (*guiri*) and natural human feelings (*ninjô*)', a conflict that
was enhanced by Kabuki theatre.[49] Etymologically, the word Kabuki derives
from the verb *kabuku* (to deviate, to be unconventional), making its performers
famous as 'eccentric and showy beings', and even having been banned in 1629,
and again in 1652, for being associated with prostitution.[50] Other authors argue
that the name comes from the fact that the word is written with the ideograms
of singing (*ka*), dancing (*bu*) and action (*ki*).[51]

Unlike the minimalism of Noh, Kabuki is characterized by its 'stylized
realism', clearly different from the Western one, sometimes falling into
exaggeration, where performers who interpret eccentric female roles stand
out.[52] This markedly performative aspect of the actors would be an inspiration
for Paulo Rocha: 'It was also the case of the Kabuki Theatre, later on, in which
the actor's body is an emitter of energies, both sonorously and in other ways
too.'[53] He adds: 'The end of the shot [69] is pure Kabuki theatre, with two bodies
standing still and framing each other, in a *mie*, in a pose radiating energy.
The only thing missing is the cries of the audience applauding the actors.'[54]
Rocha also recalls that Kabuki was a reference in terms of 'marking actors and
exaggerating certain spectacular elements, clothes, positions, colours, sounds
that become music', but also the time of the narrative ('The Kabuki journey can
start at eleven in the morning and end at nine at night') and its organization
('What you will see is not a play with a beginning, a middle and an end, but a
series of half-hour acts or fragments or an hour').[55]

---

[46]   Rocha, *Rio do Ouro*, p. 98.
[47]   Rocha, *Rio do Ouro*, p. 99.
[48]   Rocha, *Rio do Ouro*, p. 92.
[49]   Kusano, *Teatro Tradicional Japonês*, p. 9.
[50]   Kusano, *Teatro Tradicional Japonês*, p. 12.
[51]   Kusano, *Teatro Tradicional Japonês*, p. 12.
[52]   Kusano, *Teatro Tradicional Japonês*, p. 12.
[53]   Rocha, *Rio do Ouro*, p. 92.
[54]   Rocha, *Rio do Ouro*, p. 103.
[55]   Rocha, *Rio do Ouro*, p. 87.

In scenic terms, Kabuki was more exuberant than Noh, with 'a wide variety of painted scenarios and rapid changes of scenery in public view', with a catwalk (*hanamichi*) that allowed interaction with the audience and, from the eighteenth century, with a revolving stage and ceiling.[56] This seems to have been the inspiration for the kaleidoscopic skylight that dominates Canto II of the film *A Ilha dos Amores*: 'It is one of the moments in the film where the decor works best, as one of the characteristics of the skylight is to have four completely identical faces, which makes the pans and reflections in the mirrors create an infinite virtual space.'[57]

And there are also other sound influences in the film from Kabuki: 'This was one of the scenes [shots 73 and 74] in which the Kabuki aesthetic should have been more present, especially with regard to the background sound and the music. In Kabuki, the noise of the actors' footsteps on the wooden floor and the use of isolated musical notes to link syllables or phrases of the actors, produce a sound continuum that is different, for example, from that of opera, in which the phrase sung is longer'.[58]

In short, Rocha proposes that the viewing experience of *A Ilha dos Amores* could also be similar to that provided by Kabuki theatre: 'if people are tired or don't like what comes next, they go to the theatre restaurant to eat, drink, smoke, chat with friends, until the actor or act that interests them appears.'[59] More than these specific Japanese theatrical styles, Rocha sought to explore 'a compromise between various forms of performance: vaudeville, auto, musical, comic entertainment, etc.',[60] merging theatrical expressions from East and West in an attempt to create something new, transcivilizational, that would step outside its specific civilizational matrices.

Other Arts

Paulo Rocha would recognize that the 'aggressively modernist air' of the film's script 'scared' the Japanese members of the technical and artistic team of *A Ilha dos Amores*. For example, among multiple references, Rocha admits remnants of the expressionist cinema of the film *The Cabinet of Dr. Caligari* (1920) in shot 22 of *A Ilha dos Amores*: 'with the shadows on the clouds painted on the poorly stretched canvas'.[61]

But there are also references to another avant-garde movement in Europe at the beginning of the twentieth century: '[The skylight of Canto II] resembled a cubist space, each line could be seen in many ways and each marking pointed to

---

56 Kusano, *Teatro Tradicional Japonês*, p. 13.
57 Rocha, *Rio do Ouro*, p. 92.
58 Rocha, *Rio do Ouro*, p. 104.
59 Rocha, *Rio do Ouro*, p. 87.
60 Rocha, *Rio do Ouro*, p. 104.
61 Rocha, *Rio do Ouro*, p. 91.

many sides, so the second, third, fourth viewing always offered new readings'.[62] There is also the presence of Luís Buñuel: 'It is one of the rare occasions in the film when there will be a cinephile memory [...] that comes consciously from the same *Olvidados* by Buñuel.'[63] Another example is the fire at the end of the film: 'The fire is "Frankensteinian", it comes from those burlesque or horror films in which the setting is destroyed at the end, 'ritually'.[64]

According to Paulo Rocha himself, Mizoguchi, Renoir, Dreyer and Manoel de Oliveira were the filmmakers 'who most influenced me, but there are almost no cinephile quotes' in *A Ilha dos Amores*, but above all some 'unconscious echoes, distilled over the years, years of classic Japanese cinema.'[65] Rocha gives an example: 'At the time of shooting this six- or seven-minute shot, [...] Manuel de Oliveira and the long sequence shots of *Amor de Perdição* [1978] had not yet appeared. Were they already on the editing table? Although a friend and admirer of Manuel, I had no idea of the big changes he was preparing.'[66]

The Japanese Kôzô Okazaki (1919–2005) was the camera operator in the shootings carried out in Japan, and a very important visual influence on the film. At the age of about sixty, Okazaki was an experienced and recognized film technician with forty years of experience, who had previously worked with Josef von Sternberg (*Anatahan*, 1953), Sydney Pollack (*The Yakuza*, 1974) and Masaki Kobayashi (*Kaseki*, 1974), among many others, so he had experience of the different ways of filming in Japan and Hollywood.

Rocha recalls the importance of Okazaki during the shooting:

> Kozo Okazaki was almost an oracle: if at the end of the shot there was a smiling face, the shot was done. It was what could be called the 'absolute look'. He had forty years of experience and a first-rate dramatic mind.
>
> A European cameraman would never have such confidence in his own instinct. Okazaki is one of those legendary figures from the golden years of Japanese cinema.
>
> For a foreigner it is almost always a 'tragedy' to work with the great Japanese cinematographers. The shock is inevitable, and they end up with ulcers, swearing never again, as the spirit of traditional Japanese architectural forms is so strong that most of the frames used in Western cinema there are absurd. Dramas were therefore expected on the *Ilha*'s plateau.
>
> We were lucky, the shots seemed to film themselves. I worked with Kozo Okazaki and it was a honeymoon.[67]

Opera was also a key reference in *A Ilha dos Amores*: 'Without these humble choristers from S. Carlos, this island would not have existed.'[68] The São

[62]   Rocha, *Rio do Ouro*, p. 92.
[63]   Rocha, *Rio do Ouro*, p. 100.
[64]   Rocha, *Rio do Ouro*, p. 114.
[65]   Rocha, *Rio do Ouro*, p. 108.
[66]   Rocha, *Rio do Ouro*, p. 112.
[67]   Rocha, *Rio do Ouro*, pp. 84–85.
[68]   Rocha, *Rio do Ouro*, p. 91.

Carlos that Rocha refers to as fundamental to the making of his film is the
Portuguese Opera House of São Carlos, in Lisbon. Inaugurated on 30 June
1793, by Queen D. Maria I, it has been the home, since 1943, of the Choir of São
Carlos, which interprets the great operatic and choral-symphonic repertoire.
Rocha considered that there was 'a close relationship between the figuration of
S. Carlos at the time and the figuration of historical painting', bringing opera
closer to painting, having been a challenge to his 'imagination to create some
of the key scenes of the film'.[69]

As a work that brings together theatre and music, modern opera emerged in
Italy, in the transition from the sixteenth to the seventeenth century, standing
out for its unnatural character (where people sing instead of talking).[70] Over the
centuries, opera became an international, itinerant phenomenon, particularly
popular in France, Spain (and the colonial territories in Latin America),
England (and the United States of America), Russia (in the eighteenth century)
and Germany (with a peak in the nineteenth century), mainly due to the social
and economic power of its promoters, benefiting from 'the rigid social bonds
and hierarchies that characterized the early modern experience'.[71] Over the
centuries, opera has maintained an essentially European matrix, a reflection
of a supposed status quo and the cultural and artistic supremacy of the old
continent.

The influence of opera in *A Ilha dos Amores* is particularly important in
the scenes that make up Canto VIII: 'It is difficult to film an opera, and in our
country there is not even a tradition of creating them. Composer, actors, set
designer, for everyone it was the first time. It's a little suicidal to want to do
opera like that.'[72] On the other hand, one of the locations for some scenes in
twentieth-century Tokyo, the Ginza sequence that takes place on the terrace
of a building, was chosen because the neo-classical style of the Wako house
'resembles one of those settings from avant-garde plays and operas in Berlin at
the beginning of the twentieth century'.[73]

The revaluation of the scenic space, the 'idea of the stage and theatrical
space', the influence of classical painting ('the great murals, the Sistine chapel')
and the desire to break with a 'mechanical' or 'lazy' cinema, returning to a
certain mise-en-scène of silent cinema, were decisive for Rocha's recurrent use
of the long shot in *A Ilha dos Amores*:

> It allowed for a new poetics of space, of the actor's body and voices, of the
> text... As the rules were discovered, a new type of 'generalized montage'
> appeared, a form of collage within a rather long shot, making it explode,

[69] Rocha, *Rio do Ouro*, p. 91.
[70] Donald Jay Grout and Hermine Weigel Williams, *A Short History of Opera* (New York: Columbia University Press, 2003), p. 2.
[71] Louise Stein, 'How Opera Traveled', in *The Oxford Handbook of Opera*, ed. by Helen M. Greenwald (Oxford: Oxford University Press, 2015), pp. 843–84.
[72] Rocha, *Rio do Ouro*, p. 109.
[73] Rocha, *Rio do Ouro*, p. 91.

and producing dozens or hundreds of small ruptures and echoes or internal rhymes, of narrative fragments that were brought together within the same shot, either by the movement of the camera or by the displacement of the actors in the setting and that created a game of mirrors, relations of complicity or 'allergy' between parts of images, bodies, words, sounds, pushing each isolated point in the temporal flow to the brink.[74]

Western Renaissance painting was also a conscious influence for Rocha:

Putting Luís in the background, walking on the waves, between the oars and the painted dolphins, with Clara weaving barefoot among the oarsmen, in the manner of Botticelli's 'Spring' — in a take that was almost five minutes long — was certainly tempting fate.[75]

Dance is also an artistic expression that enhances the encounter between East and West. For example, in the scene of the Death of Ko-Haru (shots 77 to 79), Rocha proposes a fusion between the 'dance of the dead of the people of Tokushima and the "Dance of Death" of the war in Europe [...]. The dance of the dead in Tokushima, the music, the roar of cannon, the mural painting with soldiers in the snow. Sounds and images, life and death, dance and war, Tokushima and Europe, forcibly merge into a single shot, harmonize with each other.'[76]

There are many more elements of West–East dialogue present in the film *A Ilha dos Amores*, most of which are isolated, circumstantial or indirect allusions, and many more would be present if it weren't for the financial or production constraints. For example: 'From Rafael [Bordalo Pinheiro] came a scene that I really wanted to do. It was "Zé Povinho" in Tokushima: Moraes has an amazing page about an orangutan that is dying in a circus in Tokushima and which puts Moraes irresistibly in mind of the Lusitanian "Zé Povinho"'.[77]

'Zé Povinho' is an 'essential caricature of the Portuguese character, of the "homo Lusitanus", although marked by a touch of burlesque and satire [...], he is Portugal, a certain Portugal or a certain psychological way to portray the Portuguese with many defects (and also some virtues) properly enhanced or caricatured, with its socio-economic backwardness.'[78] First appearing in a magazine entitled *Lanterna Mágica* in 1875, in the year that Wenceslau de Moraes finished attending the Naval Academy, the character 'Zé Povinho' was created by Rafael Bordalo Pinheiro to criticize the ruling classes of the second half of the nineteenth century and he reached the twenty-first century as the ultimate symbol of popular culture.

In a provocative way, Rocha had tried to reterritorialize the illiterate 'Zé Povinho', demonstrating that he was not only interested in erudite or elitist

---

74   Rocha, *Rio do Ouro*, p. 86.
75   Rocha, *Rio do Ouro*, p. 109.
76   Rocha, *Rio do Ouro*, p. 106.
77   Rocha, *Rio do Ouro*, p. 93.
78   João Medina, 'Rafael Bordalo Pinheiro e o Zé Povinho, auto-caricatura do Português', *Estudos Literários*, 6.11 (2005), 137–48 (p. 138).

dialogues between East and West, mainly carried out by figures at the top of the social, diplomatic or military hierarchy (such as Wenceslau de Moraes himself), but which also interests him in more popular manifestations, such as the kung-fu films produced in Hong Kong in the 1970s: 'In these films from the Bruce Lee series, other cultural roots can be detected [...]. The truth is that they are often much more brilliant than a European director of the same type'.[79]

Some Final Thoughts

Co-produced between Portugal and Japan, *A Ilha dos Amores* has a production method that distinguishes it from most international co-productions that we have known since the 1950s, such as the popular Spaghetti Westerns or the Sword-and-Sandal movies. Over these decades, 'the rise of co-productions is part of a wider narrative of financial and institutional dynamics shaping the industrial organization in the film industry'.[80]

On the one hand, Transnational cinema arises in the interstices between the local and the global, moving beyond 'the exceptionalizing discourses of "Third Worldism" and the related notion of Third Cinema', that emerged and became popular in the 1960s. On the other hand, Transnational cinema also 'problematizes "postcolonialism" as an attempt to maintain and legitimize conventional notions of cultural authenticity', providing a more 'multivalenced approach to considering the impact of history on contemporary experience'.[81]

However, Ezra and Rowden warn that, 'although it can be argued that, as a spectatorial object, each film requires a particular epistemological and referential framework in order to be "fully" readable, increasingly these frameworks are losing the national and cultural particularity they had'.[82] The reduced physical mobility of the majority of the world's population and the limited means of circulating information outside national contexts clearly restricted viewers' access to cultural references and more diverse epistemic contexts. I believe that, on an international level, *A Ilha dos Amores* is indeed one of the first truly transcivilizational filmic phenomena in the history of cinema, requiring, in order to be fully enjoyed, a cosmopolitan or transcivilizational spectator, something that was still uncommon in the early 1980s.

A Ilha dos Amores not only presents a mixture of narrative contents, of different materialities (literature, theatre, music, painting, dance, etc.), but is essentially built from a dialogue of narrative structures and forms, which are

---

[79]   Rocha, *Rio do Ouro*, p. 40.
[80]   Norbert Morawetz, Jane Hardy, Colin Haslam and Keith Randle, 'Finance, Policy and Industrial Dynamics: The Rise of Coproductions in the Film Industry', *Industry and Innovation*, 14.4 (2007), 421–43 (p. 422).
[81]   Elizabeth Ezra and Terry Rowden (eds), *Transnational Cinema: The Film Reader* (London: Routledge, 2007), pp. 4–5. About Transnational cinema, see also Mette Hjort, 'On the Plurality of Transnationalism', in *World Cinemas, Transnational Perspectives* (London: Routledge, 2010), pp. 12–33.
[82]   Ezra and Rowden, *Transnational Cinema*, p. 4.

combined in the creation of something that goes beyond the mere sum of the parts. Following the example of the personal journey of Wenceslau de Moraes and Luís de Camões, Paulo Rocha lived part of his life in the East to learn the language and culture in loco, from within. But *A Ilha dos Amores* is also the result of Paulo Rocha's travelling around the world before residing in Japan, and the possibility of cinema inventing a new world, a collage of multiple landscapes and sound territories, characters and myths, emotions and sensations.

Entre eu e Deus by Yara Costa:
An Unprecedented Representation of the
Island of Mozambique

Jessica Falconi

CEsA/ISEG Lisbon

Introduction

Filmed on the Island of Mozambique, *Entre eu e Deus* [Between God and I] (2018) is the third film by Mozambican director Yara Costa and brings an original representation of a crucial place in the Mozambican cultural imagination.

Yara Costa was born in Mozambique in 1982. She studied journalism at the Universidade Federal Fluminense in Brazil and holds a master's degree in documentary filmmaking from New York University. She later furthered her studies at the International Film School in Cuba. Recently, she founded the YC Creative Platform to develop and promote multimedia artistic projects on African cultural and natural heritage.[1] Costa's documentaries explore several topics, such as migration, identity, climate change and post-colonial societies in the Global South. Her first documentary, *The Crossing*, examines the complex relationship between Haiti and the Dominican Republic. Her second one, as I will briefly show in the first part of this article, focuses on Chinese migration to Africa. After *Entre eu e Deus*, the director released *Ruins of the River* in 2021, a poetic tribute to the Mozambican people's resilience to Cyclone Idai's effects. Costa was honoured with the French Ministry of Culture's *Courants du Monde* prize in 2023 for her project *Nakhoda and the Mermaid*. This immersive art installation serves as a powerful warning about the urgent and devastating effects of global warming on African coastal communities.[2]

This article aims to dissect the documentary *Entre eu e Deus* with the primary objective of demonstrating that the director sets out to challenge images, representations and crystallized perceptions of the Island of Mozambique, Mozambican cultural identity and Islamic fundamentalism, and that she succeeds in doing so. The article consists of two main sections. The first provides a brief historical context of the Island of Mozambique and examines

[1]   <https://www.yc-creativeplatform.org>.
[2]   <https://www.futuroscriativos.org/actualidade/artista-mocambicana-vence-premio-no-forum-de-criacao-africa-em-paris/>.

Portuguese Studies vol. 40 no. 2 (2024), doi:10.1353/port.00014, pp. 175–88
© Modern Humanities Research Association 2024

some visual representations that predate the documentary under analysis. Here, I pay particular attention to Licínio Azevedo's documentary on the Island of Mozambique as a relevant antecedent of Yara Costa's work. The second part provides a detailed analysis of *Entre eu e Deus*, demonstrating the director's unprecedented representation of the Island of Mozambique.

Antecedents: Historic and Filmic

Thanks to its ancient insertion in the interregional arena of political, economic and cultural interaction of the Indian Ocean,[3] the north of Mozambique, where the Island of Mozambique is located, was, for centuries, a part of Africa closest to the 'Orient', along with other areas on the eastern coast of Africa.[4] In particular, the Island of Mozambique acted as a focal point for the commercial, political and religious networks that linked the Mozambican coast to other shores of the Indian Ocean, such as the Comoro Islands and the sultanate of Zanzibar. Furthermore, the Island of Mozambique was the first place in the territory that would become Mozambique, where Vasco da Gama's fleet arrived in 1498. The Island gave its name to the entire territory, hence its relevance in Mozambican cultural imagery.

With the establishment of the Portuguese Empire in East Africa from the sixteenth century onwards, and the creation of the *Estado da Índia* [State of India], which 'irradiated from Goa to the western coast of the Indian Ocean and to the eastern shores of the Pacific', the 'oriental face' of Mozambique was both reinforced and enhanced.[5] Only in 1752, with the dissolution of the *Estado da Índia*, was the government of the Captaincy of Mozambique unbound from Goa (the administrative centre of the *Estado*), becoming a direct dependency of Lisbon. This also led to the transfer of the colonial capital of Mozambique from the Island of Mozambique to Lourenço Marques, further to the south. This southward movement in the political and economic colonial epicentre of Mozambique also shifted the region's status in the wider Indian Oceanic world.

From the early twentieth century, Mozambique's cultural landscape began to take on a distinctly 'oriental' character, shaped by significant migratory flows from the Indian subcontinent,[6] and China.[7] These migrations persisted despite

---

[3] Sugata Bose, *A Hundred Horizons: The Indian Ocean in the Age of Global Empire* (London and Cambridge, MA: Harvard University Press, 2006), p. 11.
[4] Mario Zamponi, 'Ilha de Moçambique: crocevia di popoli e culture nell'Oceano Indiano', in *Ilha de Moçambique: incontro di popoli e culture*, ed. by Matteo Angius and Mario Zamponi (San Marino: AIEP, 1999), pp. 11–24 (p. 11).
[5] Sandra Lobo, Jessica Falconi, Remy Dias and Dave A. Smith, 'Introduction', in *The Colonial Periodical Press in the Indian and Pacific Ocean Regions*, ed. by Sandra Lobo et al. (London: Routledge, 2023), pp. 1–35 (pp. 4–5).
[6] Nicole Khouri and Joana Pereira Leite, 'Les Indiens dans la presse coloniale portugaise du Mozambique 1930–1975', *Lusotopie*, 15.2 (2008), 3–50, doi:10.1163/17683084-01502002.
[7] Eduardo Medeiros, 'Os sino-moçambicanos da Beira: mestiçagens várias', *Cadernos de Estudos Africanos* 13/14 (2007), 1–23, <https://cea. revues.org/494>.

a shift in commercial activities from Indian Ocean trade routes to connections with the continent's interior, especially South Africa. This historical relationship with the Orient has left a lasting impression on the territory, with writers and thinkers describing Mozambique as a 'varanda sobre o Índico' [balcony over the Indian Ocean],[8] or a 'Janela para Oriente' [Window on the Orient].[9] Such imagery has inspired scholarly interest in examining the construction of orientalist representations in Mozambican literature.[10] However, Yara Costa's documentary offers a different approach: rather than reinforcing orientalist views, it presents a contemporary portrayal of the historical Portuguese Orient.

It is worth noting that the Island of Mozambique was formerly uninhabited as it was devoid of drinking water and was therefore only used during short periods for seasonal pastoral or fruit-gathering activities. Arab merchants chose the Island as a landing place and a refuge for those who were sailing north or south, or in the direction of India. With the arrival of the Portuguese, the number of Swahili and Asian merchants diminished, and the bipartite face of the city began to form: the city of stone and lime, which was inhabited by the colonial administration, and the city of *macuti*,[11] where the African and Asian population lived. When the capital of the colony was moved to Lourenço Marques, the Island of Mozambique entered a state of decay, which, *mutatis mutandis*, has continued until the contemporary era. Declared a UNESCO World Heritage Site in 1991, the Island is attempting to be reborn as a city of the Indian Ocean.

Under colonial rule and particularly after Mozambique's independence, in 1975, the Island of Mozambique's cultural representation has grappled with a key aspect of its identity, namely, its role as a hub for commercial, cultural and religious routes before and after the arrival of the Portuguese. This role contributed to the emergence of distinct and sometimes opposing representations of the Island, which were later appropriated and recreated by different discourses. On the one hand, the Island was perceived as a 'lupanar da história' [brothel of history],[12] a hellish place of slavery, and of submission to the different dominations that passed through. On the other hand, the Island projected the image of an exemplary place of peaceful coexistence between peoples and cultures, emblematic of that 'world that the Portuguese created',

---

[8]   The expression is attributed to the Portuguese philosopher Eduardo Lourenço.
[9]   The title of a book by Mozambican poet Eduardo White.
[10]   Ana Mafalda Leite and Jessica Falconi, 'Island of Mozambique: Narratives from a Contact Zone', in *Cities of the Lusophone World*, ed. by Doris Wieser and Ana Filipa Prata (Oxford: Peter Lang, 2018), pp. 69–92; Nazir Can, 'Oriente e Orientalismo na literatura moçambicana', in *Geografias literárias de língua portuguesa no século XXI*, ed. by Maria Fontes, Nazir Can and Rita Chaves (Rome: Gruppo editorial tab, 2021), pp. 233–56.
[11]   *Macuti* is the local name given to the roofs made with palm leaves, largely used for residents' homes.
[12]   António Sopa and Nelson Saúte, *A Ilha de Moçambique pela voz dos poetas* (Lisbon: Edições 70, 1992), p. 53.

which was theorized by Gilberto Freyre.[13] These representations make the Island's memory a complex and contentious heritage, shaping the disputed role it plays in Mozambique's national identity.[14]

Written and visual representations reflect the Island of Mozambique's complex historical and cultural identity. In addition, several studies have highlighted its long and constant presence in Mozambican literature from the colonial and post-independence periods and its role in representing the nation and the so-called *moçambicanidade*.[15]

In terms of audiovisual production, the Island of Mozambique was filmed several times both before and after Mozambique's independence. In colonial propaganda films, it was represented as the cradle of the history of the Portuguese Empire in the Indian Ocean and as a place that embodied the multiracial rhetoric of late colonialism;[16] after independence, it appeared in reports on Portuguese television as the ruin of a post-imperial melancholy.[17]

Without intending to reconstruct here the Mozambican and foreign filmography about the Island — a topic for future work — I believe that Licínio Azevedo's documentary *A Ilha dos Espíritos* [The Island of Spirits] (2010) deserves to be considered as a relevant antecedent to Yara Costa's films, as it constitutes a representation that challenges the hegemonic narratives that make the Island a celebratory monument to the so-called Portuguese Expansion. Such narratives privileged the historical legacy of the Portuguese presence on the Island, represented by the architectural heritage of the colonial city, with its churches and palaces.

Based on a script by writer Luís Bernardo Honwana and Licínio Azevedo himself, *A Ilha dos Espíritos* was co-produced by the Mozambican production companies Ébano and Technoserve and received the support of the *Fond Images Afrique* of the French Ministry of Foreign and European Affairs. Despite falling within a complex period of Mozambican production, generally dominated by filmmaking to commission from NGOs,[18] Azevedo's documentary constitutes a representation that aims to decolonize the Island, focusing on the spiritual and popular dimension as its striking feature. However, it is worth highlighting that this representation still relies on a crystallized image that celebrates the idea of peaceful coexistence between different identities, if not the cultural hybridity on the Island.

[13]   It is an image celebrated during the Brazilian sociologist's visit to Mozambique and the Island, as part of the longest trip through the Portuguese colonies, reported in his *Aventura e Rotina* (1953).
[14]   Rita Chaves, 'Entre as palavras e o silêncio', *Metamorfoses*, 3 (2002), 93–101.
[15]   Jessica Falconi, 'Para fazer um mar: literatura moçambicana e Oceano Índico', *Diacrítica*, 27 (2013), 77–92; Carmen Tindó Secco, 'O Índico: um oceano de multiculturalidades, imaginação literária e insularidades', *Remate de Males*, 38 (2018), 147–60.
[16]   See *Ilha de Moçambique: imagens duma velha capital histórica*, by Carlos Marques (1951), available at <http://www.cinemateca.pt/Cinemateca-Digital/Ficha.aspx?obraid=2128&type=Video>.
[17]   See, for example, *Ilha de Moçambique: à espera da monção* by Joaquim Furtado (1983), and the first episode of *Mar das Índias*, by Camilo de Azevedo (1997).
[18]   Ros Gray, *Cinemas of the Mozambican Revolution: Anti-Colonialism, Independence and Internationalism in Filmmaking, 1968–1991* (Woodbridge: James Currey, 2020), kindle edition, no pagination.

The images and speech captured by Licínio Azevedo comprise a tour passing through various points on the Island. We visualize the religious mosaic through the images portraying the mosques as well as the Catholic churches on the Island, along with the moments dedicated to the teaching of both religions. Montage and sound are used for the construction and representation of a space strongly marked by religious, cultural and linguistic polyphony. As the documentary demonstrates, in many cities of the non-western world, the religious dimension represents a critical *locus* of imagination and cultural identification, having a significant impact on the configuration of the space of the city itself.[19]

As pointed out by Ute Fendler, the documentary initially presents two parallel narratives. The first is an 'official' narrative, assembled on the basis of the depositions of a historian and a maritime archaeologist. The second is a popular narrative, based on the memory of the presence of spirits, narrated and added to by various Island dwellers, which 'steadily occupies more space, more time, in comparison with the documental part'.[20]

In this perspective, the documentary appears to put into dialogue and counterpoint the Island as *museum* and the Island as *archive*, understanding the latter as a set of representations and hegemonic discourses, produced by authorities and powers; an archive in which subaltern narratives issue as silences, hidden as much by colonial power as by the nationalistic discourse of the independent State. In gathering the memories of the places where the spirits lived and passed, the documentary tries to expose, and make visible and audible through popular discourse, that which was hidden or silenced by the *archive* and does not have access to the *museum*. It is a question of recording *subaltern pasts*;[21] that is, knowledge and memories that are not inscribed in the discourses and political, historiographic or artistic representations of the Island of Mozambique.

Another relevant aspect of this documentary is the emphasis given to the presence of the Islamic religion on the Island through various elements, such as the images and sounds of the Mosque, the daily life of Mamude, the guardian of the bridge that connects the Island to the mainland, and the shots filmed at the Koranic school. However, as I will illustrate, this is a representation of Islam quite different from that proposed by Yara Costa, as Azevedo portrays the so-called Africanized Islam, following his focus on the manifestations of the Island's cultural syncretism.

All the same, given the prominence of Licínio Azevedo in the history of Mozambican cinema, his on-screen representation of Islam in the Island of

---

[19]   Gary Bridge and Sophie Watson, 'City Imaginaries', in *A Companion to the City*, ed. by Gary Bridge and Sophie Watson (Oxford: Blackwell Publishing, 2000), pp. 7–17 (p. 8).
[20]   Ute Fendler, 'Quando os filmes convidam a viajar... cinema e/é viagem', *Cerrados*, 41 (2016), 304–12 (p. 308).
[21]   Dipesh Chakrabarty, 'Histórias de minorias, passados subalternos', in *Deslocalizar a Europa: antropologia, arte, literatura e história na pós-colonialidade* (Lisbon: Cotovia, 2005), pp. 209–31.

Mozambique constitutes a critical antecedent to Yara Costa's filmographic approach to the Island. A Brazilian filmmaker resident in Mozambique for many years, Azevedo realized a vast body of works which portray various aspects of Mozambican culture, history and society, in relation to the present as well as the recent past of the country. In general, Azevedo's films tread the paths of post-colonial cinema, a cinema that invests in the need to shatter the grand narratives, 'opening space for the infinite specificities that refract larger, often repressed, miswritten, and unofficial histories of the nation, communities, classes, genders, and subaltern groups'.[22] More specifically in relation to documentaries, Azevedo's production reveals a constant concern with both the recording of the different voices and memories that inhabit the country, and the need to reinterpret historical and cultural heritage taking into consideration the current demands of the Mozambican population.

While there are important filmic continuities between the themes and subjects in Azevedo's work and *Entre eu e Deus*, it is not the only film Yara Costa has made about the Island of Mozambique. Her second documentary film, *Why are they here? Chinese stories in Africa* (2011), deals with the lives of three Chinese emigrants living, respectively, on the Island of Mozambique, in Semonkong, Lesotho, and in Accra. The episode dedicated to the Island of Mozambique develops the general argument of the documentary, which aims to investigate the presence of Chinese people on the African continent following the migratory waves that occurred after the first conference of the Forum on China–Africa Cooperation in 2000. Segmented into four sequences, it tackles the figure of Min Nan Wang, a young Chinese man aged twenty-three who arrived on the continent in 2006 to work in the exportation of sea cucumbers to China — a country where the sea cucumber is considered a gourmet foodstuff. Although the China–Africa relationship is examined in the documentary as a recent phenomenon and current event, the exportation of sea cucumbers from the Mozambique region to Chinese and Asian markets has a much longer history,[23] one that connects the trajectory of this young man to a broader history of transcontinental relations, transits and traffic on the stage of the Indian Ocean.

The first sequence of the episode introduces the young Chinese, locating him in the context of the Island of Mozambique, thus providing a representation, albeit partial, of the location of another community, this time insular. The juxtaposing of the shots of this initial sequence points to the correlation between space and social relations, working the ideas of exterior/interior; open/closed; inclusion/exclusion. In fact, the young man is framed in an exterior space delimited by metal bars that outline the sea, while he tries, without

[22]   Sandra Ponzanesi and Marguerite Waller, *Postcolonial Cinema Studies* (New York and London: Routledge, 2012), p. 9.
[23]   Edward Alpers, 'From Littoral to Ozone: On Mike Pearson's Contributions to Indian Ocean History', *Journal of Indian Ocean World Studies*, 2.1 (2018), 12–24.

success, to talk on his mobile phone to his distant family. In the following shots, while the voice off screen refers to feelings of homesickness, a series of shots in a closed space shows moments when the inhabitants of the islands, and particularly the women, come together and socialize. The internal composition of the shots and their inter-relationship reveal a complex articulation of the binaries exterior/interior, open/closed, light/shadow. The spaces where the African women socialize are marked simultaneously by vivid colours and shadow, while the space of the young Chinese man's loneliness is open and full of light, but cut by the bars.

Attention should also be paid to the presence of a closed wooden door in both spaces, which suggests symbolically a possible opening that does not, however, materialize in the narrative. Also, the shots that depict the young man in the streets of the Island register his isolation and his lack of integration into the social fabric of the Island. This is confirmed by his testimony, which alludes to the unfriendly relations with the inhabitants of the Island, who, in his words, are afraid of the Chinese and step out their way whenever they see them in the street. Thus, for Min Nan Wang, looking lingeringly at the sea is a way for him to feel closer to his country, which transforms the ocean into a connecting link, more than separation, between countries and continents.

If this imaginary connection acquires positive connotations in the young man's discourse, the real inter-economy of which he is a mediator has impacts and problematic consequences in the insular community, as explored in the second sequence of the episode, throughout which there is a closer focus on the impact of the sea cucumber business on local sustainability. Different shots focus on the search for the sea cucumbers in the sea, showing that this is a kind of artisanal fishing, carried out through diving by individuals or small groups, with the help of little boats. Through the captions and interventions of the fishermen, the documentary depicts a fragile environmental, economic and social balance, since the sea cucumbers were once abundant along the Mozambican coast, but the growth in demand in Asia, the lack of regulation, and the illegal trade have radically altered the availability of this species beside the Island of Mozambique. According to the testimony of biologist Célia Macamo, many families from coastal locations depend on the sea cucumber business, and the current shortage puts their food security and subsistence at risk. In addition, the Mozambican fishermen complain about the conditions in which the business takes place, since the value of the cucumbers is fixed by the Chinese entrepreneurs, leaving the fishermen without a great margin for negotiation. Thus, the episode of the documentary shows how the sea cucumbers, from being organisms in the Mozambican coastal ecosystem, are transformed into transnational merchandise through the interfacing dynamics of economics, power and desire, incorporating stories of work, displacements and unequal relations, as well as the failures of the post-colonial State.

From an aesthetic point of view, what Laura Marks defines as 'haptic visuality'[24] is privileged in this documentary, as the capacity of the images to evoke tactile and, more generally, bodily sensations is explored. In fact, various shots capture the inhabitants of the Island involved in activities in which the movement of the body is central, as for example in dance; the religious rituals in the mosque; the preparation and placing of the *m'siro*,[25] and the actual diving to catch sea cucumbers. In these shots, too, the emphasis on the texture of the bodies and material recreates a universe experienced through the senses, beyond the visible and the audible.

In general, the representation of the Island of Mozambique provided in this documentary challenges and deconstructs the idea of the Island as a place of peaceful coexistence between different cultures. The social isolation of the young Chinese man and the discrimination he suffers shatter a long-held representation of the cosmopolitanism of this place. The documentary also testifies to the director's interest in focusing on little-known aspects of life on the Island, with the ethnographic and picturesque forays that filmography about the Island has accustomed us to being completely abandoned. The episode also works as part of a mosaic of perspectives on the Island that *Entre eu e Deus* comes to expand and complement, confirming a broader project of inquiry into the Island's life and its local and global dynamics.

Entre eu e Deus

When asked in an interview about the form of *Entre eu e Deus*, Yara Costa states that she is not concerned with the formal classifications of her films, such as documentary, docufiction, etc., as these categories express different ways of telling a story.[26] Her response can be read as an awareness of how the increasing fluidity to documentary modes of production and narrative boundaries, alongside the impact of technological innovations, alters perspectives and pursuits of a filmic project.[27] Indeed, the author and media scholar, John Corner, would concur with Costa: 'To ask "is this a documentary project?" is more useful than to ask "is this film a documentary?" '.[28] In sum, both hold the view that it is more productive to see documentaries as a practice than as an object, a view that encapsulates the filmic projects of Yara Costa.

It is worth noting, too, that the young director is part of a new generation of Mozambican filmmakers, such as Inadelso Cossa and Lara Sousa, among

---

[24]   Laura Marks, *The Skin of the Film* (Durham, NC, and London: Duke University Press, 2000).
[25]   Beauty mask made with natural dust.
[26]   Carmen Tindó Secco, Ana Mafalda Leite and Luís Carlos Patraquim, 'Entrevista com Yara Costa', in *Cinegrafias moçambicanas*, ed. by Carmen Tindó Secco, Ana Mafalda Leite and Luís Carlos Patraquim (São Paulo: Kapulana, 2019), pp. 129–34 (p. 131).
[27]   Thomas Austin and Wilma de Jong, 'Introduction: Rethinking Documentary', in *Rethinking Documentary: New Perspectives, New Practices*, ed. by Thomas Austin and Wilma de Jong (Maidenhead: Open University Press, 2008), pp. 1–10 (p. 1).
[28]   John Corner, 'Performing the Real: Documentary Diversions', *Television and New Media*, 3.3 (2002), 255–69 (p. 258).

others, who develop their work in a context of extreme precariousness and fragility in terms of infrastructure and support for projects.[29] In the interview already mentioned, the director regrets the absence of a national policy to support cinema and points to the insufficiency of competitions that are launched from time to time by the European Union or other institutions related to PALOP.[30] We can, therefore, interpret the lack of concern with formal categories also as a response to the concrete conditions of cinema production in Mozambique, which are heavily dependent on aid from external institutions since the dismantling of national policies and infrastructures to support the development of cinematographic and audiovisual production. In fact, *Entre eu e Deus*, which the author assumed to be a documentary, emerged as an extended version of a previous short film made as part of a competition for directors from Portuguese-speaking African Countries and East Timor. As the director herself reports in another interview,[31] there was so much filmed material that she decided to dedicate a longer project to the story of Karen, a young resident of the Island of Mozambique who adheres to radical Islam.

Although focused on a young and contemporary character, the documentary recalls the long history of the presence of Islam in Mozambique and on the Island in particular, through the initial caption, which reads:

> Islam arrived for the first time on the Island of Mozambique around the eighth century. It merged with the ancient Macua tradition, which worships ancestors, transforming itself into 'African Islam'. A new Islam — Wahhabism — is gaining young followers.

Historian Liazzat Bonate highlights that the Wahhabi version of Islam on the Island of Mozambique has its roots in colonial times. According to Bonate, 'By the mid-twentieth century, belonging to a Sufi Order and upholding Sufi ideas and practices was the most widespread Islamic identity of northern Mozambique'.[32] It was only in the last decade of Portuguese colonial domination in Mozambique that 'the authority of Sufi shaykhs came under attack from the newly arrived Islamists, identified locally as the Wahhabis, educated in Saudi Arabian Islamic universities'.[33] According to the historian, Wahhabism threatened the power of the Sufi elites installed in northern Mozambique, but colonial intervention in favour of the Sufis somehow prevented it from spreading. However, the Wahhabis' presence would strengthen from the 2000s

---

[29]   Ana Cristina Pereira, 'I'm a Free Man in a Free Country. Talk with Pedro Pimenta', in *Abrir os gomos do tempo: conversas sobre cinema em Moçambique*, ed. by Ana Cristina Pereira and Rosa Cabecinhas (Braga: UMinho Editora, 2022), pp. 201–18 (p. 216).
[30]   Carmen Tindó Secco, Ana Mafalda Leite and Luís Carlos Patraquim, 'Entrevista com Yara Costa', p. 129.
[31]   E-Global, interview with Yara Costa, 29 October 2018, <https://e-global.pt/noticias/mundo/entre-eu-e-deus/>.
[32]   Liazzat Bonate, 'Islam in Northern Mozambique: A Historical Overview', *History Compass*, 8.7 (2010), 573–93 (p. 585).
[33]   Liazzat Bonate, p. 585.

onwards, culminating in the radicalization and armed attacks that occurred from 2017 onwards in Mocímboa da Praia, a municipal town in the province of Cabo Delgado, spreading to other locations of the country and sowing terror among the inhabitants of the area. As is known, these were extremely violent attacks, carried out by a jihadist-inspired group, made up of armed young people, defenders of radical Islam and the application of Sharia. According to some analysts, the consolidation of the group and its choice of armed violence are related to a multiplicity of local and transnational factors, including, in addition to religious extremism, socioeconomic inequalities and the pressure of foreign capitalist extractivism in the region.[34]

As the director reports, the news of the armed attacks came during the film's editing phase. Hence, Yara Costa felt the need to bring this discussion to the film, incorporating the news in the opening sequence and throughout the documentary. Karen's story is thus related to and juxtaposed with the violent events in the region to provoke a reflection on radical Islam in Mozambique, possibly without judgment.[35] The intention to provide this reflection is evident in the opening sequence of the film, through the shots and the sound: while we hear and read in the subtitles news of armed attacks by Islamic groups in Nigeria, Somalia, Kenya and Mozambique, at the same time we hear the sound of the sea, and we see the peaceful image of a figure floating in the middle of the Indian Ocean. The pacifying symbolism of seawater and the threat of violence conveyed by the news thus coexist on the same plane, conveying a complex position on the film's subject from the beginning. In particular, the sound associated with close-ups of Karen's face creates the illusion that the character is also listening to the news, which we immediately realize is impossible. We are thus confronted, as spectators, by a disjunction of points of view conveyed by the combination of sound and images. In other words, positioning the viewer 'on the side of the news' while looking at Karen, who is immediately identifiable as a Muslim girl because she is swimming with her clothes on, one immediately sees an intention to question prejudices about the Islamic religion in general and fundamentalism in particular. From this perspective, the brief dialogue when Karen gets out of the sea is also significant. A child asks her, 'Are you getting baptized?', receiving the answer, 'No, I was just swimming'. This brief dialogue immediately recalls Karen's difficult position in the social, cultural and religious context of the Island, which will be explored throughout

---

[34] Salvador Forquilha and João Pereira, 'Dinâmicas da migração e o desenvolvimento da insurgência jihadista no Norte de Moçambique', in *Desafios para Moçambique 2022*, ed. by Carlos Nuno Castel-Branco, Rosimina Ali, Sérgio Chichava, Salvador Forquilha and Carlos Muianga (Maputo: Iese, 2022), pp. 38–58 (p. 38).

[35] The theme is familiar in Mozambican cultural production. In 2005, the writer João Paulo Borges Coelho published the short story 'O pano encantado' [The Enchanted Cloth] set on the Island of Mozambique to fictionalize the history of the ramifications and diversity of Islam in the North of the country, exploring the religious conflict between different views and practices of this religion. The story's ending announces violence and crime as consequences of religious extremism, functioning almost as a prophetic narrative of the jihadist group's armed attacks in Mozambique.

the documentary. Still in the 'prologue', the strategy of juxtaposing radio news about Wahhabi violence and images of Karen's face is resumed. As we watch her putting on makeup at home, we hear a voice say on the radio that 'Everybody who does this kind of butchery everywhere in the world is Wahhabi'. We remain on the side of the news, silently wondering what the young woman's position will be concerning the violence. A statement by Karen is a possible first answer to the implicit question raised by the news and by possible preconceived ideas of the viewer about Islam: 'My religion — the Muslim religion — nowadays is very distorted. Just because a fruit from that tree was not good does not mean the tree does not produce sweeter fruit.' Again, the contrast between the violence conveyed by the news and the imaginary of 'sweetness' evoked by the character's comment highlights the importance of developing more nuanced views on radical Islam in Mozambique and the world. Later in the documentary, we hear Karen openly comment, in a telephone conversation with a friend, on the media reports about terrorism. For the young woman, terrorists are not true Muslims, but common thinking cannot escape this sometimes simplistic association. An individual point of view on the issue thus emerges, expressing the desire to deconstruct stereotypes and preconceived ideas.

Just like Licínio Azevedo's documentary, *Entre eu e Deus* delves into the religious, cultural and spiritual dimension of the Island through brief shots of the main places of worship and cultural manifestations: we see, in sequence, the central mosque, frequented by the sect sunni; the popular dance of a group of Macua women; the Hindu temple; the evangelical church of the Assembly of God; and the Catholic church Nossa Senhora da Misericórdia. On the one hand, these shots testify to what Corner defines as a constant characteristic of documentaries: 'the *pictorial creativity*, the organization of its visual design'.[36] On the other hand, the shots in question have the function of briefly illustrating the cultural and social context in which Karen is inserted. Shortly afterwards, Karen tells a friend of a conversation with someone who had asked her if she was real, which underlines the profound perplexity of the Island's inhabitants regarding her appearance. In a telephone conversation, Karen also reports that at school, a teacher asked her to remove her headscarf, which also reinforces the perception of estrangement and, to a certain extent, discrimination suffered by the young woman. Karen also mentions some comments from colleagues who associate her clothing with violence: 'I've been called a bomb girl in class, they've said that there's a bomb inside my clothes'. The fact that Karen is a young woman and the issue of women's Islamic clothing make her religious choice and cultural difference even more striking in the context of the Island. This difference is also highlighted by the contrast with the testimony of an older Muslim woman, who claims to follow the precepts and

---

[36] John Corner, 'Documentary Studies: Dimensions of Transition and Continuity', in *Rethinking Documentary: New Perspectives, New Practices*, ed. by Thomas Austin and Wilma de Jong (Maidenhead: Open University Press, 2008), pp. 13–28 (pp. 21–22).

customs of the Africanized Islam dominant on the Island of Mozambique and among the Macua population. For this woman, the clothing rules imposed by Wahhabism are unacceptable and considered almost a denial of local culture and customs. The woman works as Karen's foil precisely because of her vision of the relationship between Islam and African tradition. It is a relationship that Karen also wonders about and has roots in religious, political and cultural debates that have always marked Islamic communities in Mozambique.[37] For the older woman, the African version of Islam will continue to exist despite external influences; for Karen, on the contrary, the problem is that Wahhabism is viewed with hostility because its true essence has not yet been understood. At the same time, however, Karen states, at the end of the documentary, that embracing Wahhabi Islam does not mean denying tradition but merely placing religious faith on a higher level. A third woman, Karen's aunt, enlightens her niece about Islam in Mozambique, living only as a denomination and not with true devotion. In conversation with her aunt, Karen is interested in how people practise Islam in Tanzania, stating that in that country, the religion is more authentic, different from the Mozambican case.

The documentary thus provides a diverse range of women's perceptions, ideas and experiences. In this way, we realize that the director focuses on the issue of gender as an essential and not a casual aspect of the story portrayed, articulating it with the issue of religious identity to provide a less known and discussed point of view on radical Islam. There is no doubt that in current thinking, in the media, and the dominant interpretation, Islamic fundamentalism has an eminently masculine connotation,[38] so we are faced with a less common story that fits into this phenomenon. Karen's comments on the condition of women in Islam clarify this position and explain the documentary's title. For the young woman, the 'submission' attributed to Muslim women by common thought is a distortion. She claims that many men use this common thought to exert power over women. Nevertheless, such submission does not concern men, only God: 'This is a relationship between God and me'. It is essential to highlight that these comments by Karen are associated with images of female objects and clothing, seeming to underline that female identity is a central feature in the construction of Karen's religious identity and not a renunciation of this identity, according to orientalist stereotypes about submissive Muslim women. In fact, several shots in the documentary highlight attention to clothing, makeup and body healing, seeming to want to construct, on the one hand, a feminine aesthetic generally little associated with Muslim women. On the other hand, these shots reconfirm the director's tendency towards 'haptic visuality' already explored in her first documentary, that is, an ability to evoke sensorial experiences through the

---

[37] Liazzat Bonate, 'Traditions and Transitions: Islam and Chiefship in Northern Mozambique ca. 1850–1974', (unpublished PhD thesis, University of Cape Town, 2007), p. 24.
[38] Aleksandra Dier and Gretchen Baldwin, 'Masculinities and Violent Extremism' (New York: International Peace Institute, 2022), <https://www.ipinst.org/2022/06/masculinities-and-violent-extremism>.

texture of materials and objects, rather than through their shape, which creates a general effect of great intimacy with the character.

If, on the one hand, the objective of the documentary is to portray Karen's story to discuss her option for Islamic radicalism, on the other hand, this discussion does not take place on a merely ideological level. There is also an intimate approach to the character, who reports her evolution and confesses feelings of loss about her previous identity. This dimension of intimacy is a striking feature of the documentary, resulting, on the one hand, from the close relationship between the director and the protagonist. As Yara Costa has stated in several interviews, at the time of filming, she had known Karen for many years and could follow her evolution. On the other hand, it is possible to see this dimension as a relevant trend in documentary production aimed at a process of 'intimization' of content conveyed by new forms of digital production.[39] This intimacy is conveyed at a narrative and aesthetic level through camera movements that gradually and in a contained way approach the character's body. For the director, the fact that the team and characters are all women gave the documentary a more feminine dimension, which manifests itself precisely in the intimacy and affection that permeate the entire documentary. At a narrative level, the dimension of affection is also a territory explored by Karen's reports regarding her relationship with her mother, a Mozambican woman of Macua ethnicity who worked as a model in Brazil and died before her daughter's conversion to Islam. She is present in the film through a framed photograph hanging on a wall with which Karen seems to be in silent dialogue, reactivating both an emotional closeness and a distance in terms of lifestyles and identity options. 'I ended up following a different path than her, I wasn't brought up to be Muslim... My mother always wanted me to be freer. I think she wanted me to decide, when I grew up I would really decide what I wanted to be', says Karen, seeking to affirm her difference and reconcile herself with the feeling of loss. The way her mother would probably view Karen's religious choice is a topic that the protagonist talks about at various points in the documentary, representing a territory that is sometimes painful and without definitive answers, which contributes to exploring Karen's personality and choice in a nuanced way, without giving in to the temptation of representing a monolithic and crystallized identity. Karen remains in her youth and ambivalence, aware that what she has learned about radical Islam is something that comes from outside. In the final scenes of the documentary, we again see Karen's body lying on the waves of the Indian Ocean in an open general shot which points to a possible future of these characters and of the Island itself in its relationship with the world, that is, its connection with other spaces marked by radical Islam.

Another aspect to highlight from the documentary is the relationship between character and space. If, on the one hand, we follow Karen in her daily life, at home, in the market, and in other places on the Island, what stands out

---

[39] Thomas Austin and Wilma de Jong, 'Introduction: Rethinking Documentary', p. 1.

is a dimension of isolation about her context. In this regard, several shots filmed on the beach or in the fortress of São Sebastião, which is a powerful symbol of the Portuguese Expansion in East Africa, highlight this solitary dimension that is often filled by communication technologies: conversations on the cell phone, watching videos or joining social networks. This is a dimension that permeates the entire documentary, creating a new representation of the Island's openness to the world, no longer through the intense material circulation of people but over the connections established through technology. As Karen states, everything she learned about the Islamic religion was through YouTube.

Conclusions

The story of the young Chinese man reported in the first documentary and the story of Karen and her religious choice have the merit of revealing unprecedented aspects of life on the Island of Mozambique and deconstructing the myth of the Island as a place of peaceful coexistence between different cultures. In its small space, the Island appears to be where identity conflicts occur, discrimination occurs, and the most pressing cultural differences are not readily accepted. Thus, Yara Costa's productions definitively bury the Island's Luso-tropical myth, revealing its lesser-known face. At the same time, her documentary practice investigates contemporary phenomena that have their roots in the Island's historical and cultural past, providing a complex portrait of this place and its combination of local factors and global dynamics. Both the Chinese migration and the spread of Wahhabism put in question the past, present and future of the Island and its role as a symbol of Mozambican cultural identity, increasingly fragmented by various axes of differentiation — by gender, origin and religion, among others.

Inserting itself into the tradition of documentary cinema in Mozambique, always attentive to the country's social, cultural and economic issues, Yara Costa's production is in dialogue with representations and images from the past whilst seeking to establish new places of enunciation and renew the perception of the Island in its connections with other spaces and other dynamics, reconfirming, in the end, the central role of this place in narrating contemporary Mozambican times.

East Timor in Margarida Gil's *Bitter Flowers*: The Power of the Unrooted Underdog

ANA ISABEL SOARES

CIAC / Universidade do Algarve

Flores Amargas [*Bitter Flowers*] (1989) is a medium feature made for television and Margarida Gil's fifth film. It appeared after Gil had released her first feature film for the big screen, *Relação Fiel e Verdadeira* [*True and Faithful*] (1987) and a documentary series for television, *Olho de Vidro: Uma História da Fotografia* [*Glass Eye: A History of Photography*] codirected with António Sena (1979 to 1982). *Bitter Flowers* originated from a commission by the Portuguese State TV broadcast company (RTP) for a series of television programmes, *Fados*, achieving 'o casamento do Cinema com a Televisão' [the marriage of TV and Cinema].[1] This combination is at the core of much of the director's work[2] — in the particular case of *Bitter Flowers*, it was clear that Margarida Gil wanted to set a personal point of view on a topic that was not central to the concerns of the average Portuguese citizen, but which she deemed relevant. The film responded to the need Gil identified for a Portuguese awareness or awakening to the problem of East Timor; the television format served this aim.

The territory now known as Timor Lorosa'e and officially designated Repúblika Demokrátika Timór-Leste was a Portuguese colony from the early sixteenth century when Portuguese merchants arrived on the Eastern side of the island, in 1512. East Timor was inhabited by the Mambai, who the colonizers

---

[1] 'Uma série para lembrar e que, ao abrigo do protocolo SEC/RTP, permitiu que realizadores, tanto da RTP como do exterior, dessem curso a experiências de diferentes linhas estéticas, contando, sobretudo, com meios mais largos que os habituais' [A series to be remembered, which, under a protocol between the Secretary of State for Culture and Portuguese Television, allowed directors both of RTP and others to follow different experiments in diverse aesthetic lines, most notably counting on larger funding than usual]. Fernando Lopes was the head of this project and he defined it as filling a void in Portuguese fiction to work with current topics, its goal being to 'esboçar imagens dos nossos gostos quotidianos, situações que digam qualquer coisa ao espectador' [sketch images of our routine tastes, situations that speak straight to the viewer] therefore evading the tendency 'que as ficções se passassem todas numa grande cidade, de forma a tocar outros aspectos da vida portuguesas' [to locate all fictions in a big city, and addressing other aspects of the Portuguese life], Vasco H. Teves, 'Produção Nacional: Uma aposta ganha', in *RTP: 50 Anos de História* (Lisbon: RTP, 2007), p. 13 <https://museu.rtp.pt/livro/50Anos/ Livro/DecadaDe80/ProducaoNacionalUmaApostaGanha/Pag13/default.htm>. All translations into English are my own unless otherwise indicated.
[2] I attempt to show this in my analysis of Gil's fictional and non-fictional work. See Ana I. Soares, 'Four Decades on Screen: The Fiction Films of Margarida Gil', in *Women's Cinema in Contemporary Portugal*, ed. by Mariana Liz and Hilary Owen (London: Bloomsbury, 2020), pp. 43–62, and *Margarida Gil: quatro décadas de audiovisual* (Famalicão: Editora Húmus, 2021).

Portuguese Studies vol. 40 no. 2 (2024), doi:10.1353/port.00015, pp. 189–201

called Maubere. It took more than four and a half centuries for the country to be able to declare its independence, which eventually happened at the end of 1975. However, in early December that year, East Timor was invaded by Indonesian forces and annexed as one of the country's provinces. As the first state in the world to affirm its sovereignty in the twenty-first century, East Timor gained back its independence, acknowledged internationally in May 2002, upon a Self-Determination Act supported by the United Nations, and after the Indonesian government had left the territory in 1999. This came about in the aftermath of the death of the Indonesian president Suharto (1967–98), whose men (mostly Muslim) persecuted, tortured, and terrorized the East Timorese (predominantly Catholic).

Margarida Gil's work is therefore to be understood among the complexity of Western perspectives on East Timor, namely the intricate gaze the former colonizer directs at the historically oppressed Timorese. *Bitter Flowers* represents that gaze, primarily because it is set and shot in and from the outskirts of Lisbon, former capital of a colonial empire which started to disintegrate in 1822, with the independence of Brazil, and which was the originary site of the Democratic Revolution of 1974. In that contemplation the film offers a truly essential, self-critical viewpoint that was not common in the 1980s and is still not frequently found in the Portuguese audiovisual context.

I expect to further show the extent to which Margarida Gil's knowledge of William Shakespeare's play *The Tempest*, a work with profound meaning in the discussion of Western colonialism, is particularly revealed in *Bitter Flowers* through the representation of a Portuguese 'devil' portrayed very much like Shakespeare's Caliban; in other words, in the film the colonizer (the Portuguese) is embodied in a monster-like character that shares traits with the one used by the Bard — after Michel de Montaigne's essay 'On Cannibals' — to embody the misunderstood indigenous *cannibal-Caliban* in the play.[3]

East Timor, a very particular locus in faraway Asia, with its geography visually represented in the film by a plywood scenario in a poor ballroom in the Portuguese capital, is indirectly portrayed through the demonstration of the Timorese cultural and historical traditions (music, dance, costumes), creating a filmic atmosphere that brings the country, its history, culture, and people to the fore while directing sharp criticism at the colonizer.

As a geographical location, East Timor stands among the farthest settlements of the Portuguese. In practical terms, this fact alone determined the relationship between the metropolis and the colonized territory — well into the twentieth century, Portugal being one of the few remaining European colonizers, it looked upon its old colony with something of an ashamed indifference. The medium feature film directed by Margarida Gil at the turn of the 1990s aims at overcoming that indifference by looking straight into the eyes of the Timorese

---

[3]   Interestingly, Shakespeare's play premiered in London in 1611, practically one century after Portugal colonized East Timor.

people then living as refugees in Lisbon. The then recent succession of events is summarized by journalist Adelino Gomes at the outset of the film just before the title, upon a world map showing that part of Asia with the camera zooming in on the island of Timor:

> A Indonésia invadiu Timor-Leste em 7 de dezembro de 1975. A guerra e a fome mataram duzentas mil pessoas e a ilha tornou-se numa imensa prisão. Treze anos depois, num clima de generalizada indiferença internacional, guerrilheiros resistem ainda nas montanhas. [...] Cerca de quinze mil timorenses fugiram para o exterior. A maior parte ficou na Austrália. Para a antiga metrópole vieram dois mil. Vivem em condições difíceis em Setúbal e nos arredores de Lisboa, Cacém, Amadora, Queluz, e nas casas de madeira do Campo dos Balteiros, Vale do Jamor.

> [Indonesia invaded East Timor on 7 December 1975. War and famine killed 200,000 people turning the island into a gigantic prison. Thirteen years after that, among generalized international indifference, guerrilla people still resist in the mountains. [...] Some 15,000 Timorese people fled abroad. The majority settled in Australia; two thousand came to the former metropolis, where they dwell in dire conditions in Setúbal and in the outskirts of Lisbon — Cacém, Amadora, Queluz, and in the wooden sheds at Campo dos Balteiros, Vale do Jamor.]

In 1989, Campo dos Balteiros (or 'Quinta do Balteiro') in Vale do Jamor, one of the districts in the metropolitan area of Lisbon, was still home to a significant community of Timorese refugees. Margarida Gil chose this community to locate and symbolize the Timorese people, represented as living in the land of and among the former colonizer. Adopting a hybrid tone between fiction and documentary, Gil's approach to the Timorese community alternates between anthropologically documenting the habits of the individuals living in Vale do Jamor and following a fictional plot centred on a young refugee about to leave for Timor to join the guerrillas and his younger brother who looks up to him as a hero — all sustained by dramatic dialogues which include Timorese chanting, food recipes, sports rules, traditional verse, and even lines from the work of the Portuguese poet Ruy Cinatti (who started his poetic opus after his holidays spent in the former colonies in 1935). Most of this linguistic material is in Portuguese, but Tétum makes its occasional appearance to underline relevant narrative points. The language of the colonizer is paradoxically perceived by the Timorese as a symbol of resistance vis-à-vis the Indonesian invader.[4] Timor and the Timorese are thus audiovisually represented as a culture, a synthesis of historic events understood and literally seen by the camera of a Portuguese in Portuguese territory. Historical paradoxes — in which the first colonizer is

---

[4] For more information on this, see Geoffrey Gunn's article on language and the construction of East Timor's identity, as well as Taur Matan Ruak's note on the importance of the Portuguese language for the East Timorese resistance: Geoffrey Gunn, 'Língua e Cultura na construção da identidade de Timor-Leste', *Revista Camões*, 14 (2001), 14–24; Taur Matan Ruak, 'A importância da língua portuguesa na resistência contra a ocupação indonésia', *Revista Camões*, 14 (2001), 40–41.

the documented protector but symbolically presented both as guardian and as offender — come up in a succession throughout the film, only to stress the harshness and absurdity of all colonialisms.

The East Timorese appear in the film dislocated from their homeland, attempting to make themselves at home in the land of the first occupier, but hardly succeeding. José de Matos-Cruz recalls that the title of the film is 'o nome de um ritual timorense que simboliza o tempo em que a alma se separa do corpo' [the name of an East Timorese ritual symbolizing the period when the soul separates from the body].[5] A poem collected by Fernando Pires and Emanuel Braz in East Timor establishes the dichotomy between 'sweet' and 'bitter' flowers, and reveals their interchangeability. The sweet flower 'goes on the grave' and is the 'food for the souls | Of those departed'; it becomes sweet 'When prepared by the hands | Of women who chew betel nut | And remember the loved one | Laid to rest'. The bitter flower 'is the Flower | That goes on the grave | On the seventh day | The sign of sorrow | For those who stay'. The former is an offering to the dear departed and 'marks the beginning | Of the time to let go | To hold on to the memory | To let go of the grief'; but in the end 'Bitter is the flower | That becomes sweet' and 'Sweet is the Flower | When the soul is at rest'.[6]

Bitterness is mostly felt by those who stay and mourn their dead. In Margarida Gil's film, the presence of the East Timorese soul — represented by those who survived and by their memories of the ones who fell — can only be suggested, always in search of its embodiment, but frustrated at the fact that it cannot find it where the body dwells. Some ten minutes before the end of the film (at 00:44:45), a young woman talks to a young man about to leave to fight in East Timor. She asks him why he wants to leave and he replies: 'Porque não tenho nada a ver com isto' [Because I have nothing to do with this here]. As she responds 'Nem eu — nenhum de nós' [Nor me — nor any of us], the camera turns to a young boy, Angelino, leaving the scene and stretching the argument to its paroxysm: 'Ninguém tem nada a ver com isto' [Nobody has anything to do with this]. Yet, the fact is they need to remain, as the young man affirms: 'Mas vão ficando — quantos anos queres ficar? Uns dez? Vinte?' [And yet one stays — how many years do you want to stay? Maybe ten? Twenty?]; and the woman replies: 'Os que forem necessários' [As many as necessary].

The forced indirectness of the representation of the East Timorese people turns *Bitter Flowers* into a film which is as much about that distant people as it is about Portugal's awareness of its place and role among them, their society, their past, and their culture. In a sense, the camera acts as the Portuguese gaze onto a people once subdued by Portugal, which now perceives the richness of

---

[5] José de Matos-Cruz, 'Timor e o cinema', *Revista Camões*, 14 (2001), 162–71 (p. 168).
[6] Richard Tanter, Mark Selden and Stephen R. Shalom (eds), *Bitter Flowers, Sweet Flowers: East Timor, Indonesia, and the World Community*, War and Peace Library (Oxford: Rowman & Littlefield, 2001), p. v.

their culture and the sheer injustice of colonialism. The viewer never totally faces the *otherness* of the East Timorese other, but rather stands at the threshold of its representation, as an uninvited guest who has prepared a meal and wishes to join the celebration. This is one possible reading of the many images of thresholds and doors ajar which punctuate the film; or the reason Margarida Gil chose to film so often in *plongée* shots, directing the camera towards the bare feet or the shoes of the East Timorese.

After Adelino Gomes' voice has narrated the short history of Timor and the camera has stopped at the mapped area above Australia, what appears on the screen is a natural setting of exuberant vegetation: with no internal evidence so far, the viewer could imagine herself within the mountains of East Timor. Indeed, the information needed to identify the location is not given at the start (Lisbon is vaguely mentioned, and the roar of Formula 1 engines suggests the vicinity of the Estoril Circuit); just as the names of characters and the kinship among them will only be explained to the spectator progressively through the film. By choosing to shoot the exterior scenes mostly at night and surrounded by this exuberant, virtually exotic vegetation — and by working the soundtrack to stress the wild trait of the *locus* — Margarida Gil tries to re-enact the environment of the remote mountains of East Timor at Quinta do Balteiro in Oeiras, Portugal. The same is attempted with the illustration of the Timor mountains as backdrop for the stage in the ballroom where a great portion of the plot unfolds. This displaced, wild landscape, the film seems to suggest, is the locus of memories; it is the abode of beauty, of passion, of family bonding and of trans-generational communication. Very near the end, a group of four girls recites a chanted charm about the land and the country:

[1ª] Vi a mãe ao pé do berço, por isso sei o que é o amor. Vi os olhos infantis, por isso sei o que é a fé.

[2ª] Contemplei um arco-íris, por isso sei o que é beleza. Olhei o mar agitado, por isso sei o que é o poder.

[3ª] Uma árvore plantei, por isso sei o que é a esperança. Ouvi as aves silvestres, já sei o que é a liberdade.

[4ª] Perdi um amigo, por isso sei o que é a dor. Lutei e matei na guerra, por isso sei o que é o inferno.

[Todas] Vimos e sentimos tudo isto porque sabemos que deus é o poder, amor, fé, esperança de Timor na luta pela sua liberdade.

[[First girl] I have seen the mother beside the baby's crib; therefore, I know what love is. I have seen the eyes of a child; therefore, I know what faith is.

[Second girl] I have contemplated a rainbow; therefore, I know what beauty is. I have gazed at the wild sea; therefore, I know what might is.

[Third girl] A tree I have planted; therefore, I know what hope is. I have heard the forest fowl; I already know what freedom is.

[Fourth girl] I have lost a friend; therefore, I know what pain is. I have fought and killed in the war; therefore, I know what hell is.

[All] We have seen and felt all this because we know that God is the might, the love, the faith, and the hope of Timor in its plight for freedom.]

This chant occurs outside, next to the gigantic roots of a tree, which — together with the children reciting it — suggests the ideal rooting of a solid will, the force of desiring a free, sovereign nation. It would take over a decade after the film was completed for that dream to become true for East Timor, but it is definitely significant that this idea is so enduringly imprinted on Margarida Gil's work as a message to the future.

The wilderness is, however, also the place of battle and that of death: this much is hinted at from the outset of *Bitter Flowers*, when the scene opens in broad daylight into a courtyard where men in East Timorese costumes attend a cockfight between two roosters, and place financial bets (it is only following the images of this fight that the title of the film is shown, and the narrative, so to speak, is set forth). It will be outdoors too, among the dusky atmosphere and vegetation, after Angelino descends from the tree where he was perched looking over at the events happening just outside the ballroom door, that he will fight the Portuguese 'devil' and be killed. The blood shed by the angelic boy will add to the river of blood shed by the East Timorese throughout history in the confrontation with occupants of the territory — eerily, Angelino's death anticipates the Santa Cruz Massacre in East Timor on 12 November 1991, a violent shooting by Indonesian forces who killed mostly pro-independence young men demonstrating in the Santa Cruz cemetery after a funeral mass celebrating Sebastião Gomes, a young member of the resistance movement. In the character of Angelino, *Bitter Flowers* signifies all bloodshed in fights for independence; in the evil Portuguese drunkard, it symbolizes all cowards (the man runs away upon realizing he has killed the boy), all prejudiced people (in many scenes the drunkard directs offensive remarks at a young woman's boyfriend). When he is thrown out of the ballroom by another Portuguese, he keeps insulting the others with foul words, calling them 'whores, fags, and *monhés*' (an offensive word used by Portuguese to designate Hindus). Meanwhile the good Portuguese barman is heard saying that 'Mauberes are princes', but the drunkard shouts 'S*** to the Mauberes!'). This Portuguese devil represents the injustice of oppressors, as he comes to the dance uninvited, drinks separately, and is cruelly — even fatally — unthankful. He is Prospero turned into Caliban.

The interiors, in turn, appear in the film predominantly in four specific spaces. The ballroom, where a collective celebration is taking place, is divided into three main areas: the bar, the disc-jockey's mixing table, and the stage with the painted scenario, which gains narrative relevance in the course of the film. Some scenes show those attending the ball laughing, or simply sitting on chairs by the walls. The scenes set in these areas provide the bulk of the documentary elements of the film: the camera stands mostly still, observing and showing; the gaze assumes itself as anthropological, with no intervention or comment. The context of the dance is also where the medium feature film takes a metafilmic stance, from 00:16:06 until 00:16:17, when the boy preparing the dance floor points a light projector onto Domingas, stressing not just the attention he is offering her, but also the particularly tender gaze Margarida Gil dedicates her and other women throughout the feature: the feminine figures represent hope, the smiles of a future free land. Women gather and cook in the kitchen, passing on their ancient ways (and criticizing the Portuguese produce while at it). Antonio's bedroom, another significant indoor space, has a notable window that works as a door to Angelino — as an angel, he does not tread on the floor but is often on a higher spatial level. This bedroom will serve as a changing room for Domingas, as she enters it carrying a dress just woven by an older woman in another room of the building while a puppy plays around. The camera shows the young woman entering the bedroom where Lio is lying and smoking. The girl smiles at him and opens a folding screen behind which she will put on the dress. The scene is filled with erotic innuendo: the girl's dressing gestures are merely suggested by her going behind the screen while the spectator is shown the opposite side of the room, and the camera, located in the place of the folded screen, zooms in towards the young man's body and face smoking a cigarette and looking lewdly as the camera approaches (as if he were imagining the woman's body being undressed), and the rustle of the clothes and of the ornaments of the dress being put on is heard. This is one of the most intimate moments in the film, the indoors accentuating the intimacy between the two figures. When the girl comes out from behind the screen, beautifully clad in the newly woven red dress, her arms adorned with the typical East Timorese armband and her neck with necklaces, she asks the young man to help her hold her hair and complete the figurine with a metal head band. The romantic sound of a guitar is the only musical score, along with the noises of forest fowl — the moment is interrupted by Angelino, reality breaking in through the voice of an angel peeping in from the upper internal window, telling him: 'Lio, vai-te embora. Já estão à tua espera [Lio, go away. They are waiting for you].

The precarious housing of Quinta do Balteiro (shacks made of thin brick, wood, and zinc sheets, lacking infrastructure, as suggested by the girl collecting water in a plastic jar as the title of the film appears) harbours the miserable living conditions. But it is also indoors that the apparently harsh aggression of pop music coexists with the folk dances and harmonies of the distant land. Clear paths, as transitions between outside and inside, are walked through during the day by the Timorese — they relay moments of inter-generational learning. In turn, a barely perceptible road leads a van into the main house bringing in it 'the devil' who will 'ruin the ball'. Out of this van come two Portuguese: one is introduced to the community and to the spectator as an 'irmão de sangue' [blood brother], since he celebrated a blood pact with one of the outstanding members of the Timorese group; the other appears as a 'devil', someone who will bring disgrace into the community. As the two go inside, the 'good' Portuguese brings beer and joyfully salutes and is greeted by all; the second, the 'bad' one, chooses to stay out of the beer toast and drinks spirits instead — throughout the film, his presence is accompanied by ominous music that increases in intensity up to the tragic end he causes.

With a careful *dispositio* of its narrative elements, *Bitter Flowers* can be read as an allegory. The story is even served with a character representing the *anima* of the group, and someone who reinforces the link between generations and different cultures: Angelino, who speaks both Portuguese and Tétum. Early in the film he is wearing Western clothes, chatting outside and sharing a smoke with a friend who would rather attend the Formula 1 races heard roaring in the distance than the Timorese cockfights — 'Não sei porque é que o sangue entusiasma tanto as pessoas. A mim isso não me diz nada' [I don't know why blood excites people so much. It doesn't doing anything for me], he says — but eventually Angelino changes into traditional East Timorese attire as his speech incorporates folk chanting, becoming more and more symbolic. He idolizes the young man preparing to leave for Timor, calling him a hero, and wishing to be like him. Angelino is the one coming through Lio's bedroom window and asking him to become his brother: 'Quero ser teu irmão. Pacto de sangue' [I want to be your brother. A blood pact]. The older boy replies that he is but a child: 'Um pacto é para sempre' [A pact is forever]. Angelino then draws a blade and repeats the request. The ceremony between the two is accompanied by the two reading lines from a poem Ruy Cinatti translated, duly entitled 'Poema do pacto de sangue' [Poem of the Blood Pact].[7]

This conviviality of poetry with film is a recurrent feature in Margarida Gil's works. As the camera draws closer to the boys, they settle the pact dropping

---

[7]   The poem appears as 'translated by Ruy Cinatti, Portugal/Timor' in an anthology organized by poet Sophia de Mello Breyner Andresen, who explains: 'Durante uma das suas estadas em Timor, Ruy Cinatti celebrou um pacto de sangue com o chefe de uma linhagem timorense. Por isso, daí em diante, segundo os usos e tradições de Timor, passou ele próprio a ser simultaneamente português e timorense, facto que nunca esquecia' [During one of his sojourns in Timor, Ruy Cinatti made a blood pact with the leader of a Timorese lineage. Therefore, from then on and according to the Timorese tradition Cinatti became both Portuguese and Timorese, a fact he never forgot] (p. 168). The poem represents the bond among people by way of 'un lenço velho' [an old scarf]: 'Nobres há muitos. É verdade. / Verdade. Homens muitos. É muito verdade. / Verdade que com um lenço velho / As nossas mãos foram enlaçadas. // Nós, como aliados, eu digo. / Panos, só um, tal qual afirmo. / A lua ilumina o meu feitio. / O sol ilumina o aliado. // Água de Héler! Pelo vaso sagrado! / Nunca esqueça isto o aliado. / Juntos, combater, eu quero! / Com o aliado, derrotar, eu quero! // A lua ilumina o meu feitio. / O sol ilumina o aliado. / Poderemos, talvez, ser derrotados / Ou combatidos, mas somente unidos. [There are many noblemen. That much is true. / True. Men so many. So very true. / So true that with one old scarf / Our hands have been bound. // We as many allied, I say. / Cloths, only one as I affirm. / The moon shines over my character. / The sun illuminates the allied. // Héler's water! Through the sacred vase! / May the allied never forget that. / Together, to combat I will! / With the allied to defeat I will! // The moon shines over my character. / The sun illuminates the allied. / We might perhaps be defeated / Or fought, but solely united.] (my translation). Sophia de Mello Breyner Andresen (ed.), *Primeiro livro de poesia: poemas em língua portuguesa para a infância e a adolescência* (Lisbon: Caminho, 1997), p. 168.

blood from incisions they make on each other's forearms with a blade. Angelino looks straight into the camera while Lio pronounces the last words of the poem, first in Portuguese and afterwards in Tétum. The next image shows the two making a cross with their overlapping forearms and exchanging blood. At the end of the film, Angelino's death brought about by a fight with the 'bad' Portuguese stands for the loss of innocence of a strongly bonded people subdued by centuries-long oppression.

Bitter Flowers sways elegantly from a documentary to a poetic elegy for the East Timorese people, precisely in the historical moment when the people of East Timor organize themselves and unilaterally declare their independence from the Indonesian occupier.[8] In a brief subsequent shot the spectator sees the girl peeping into the scene through a door ajar. At 00:33:19 spectators are taken back into the dance saloon: to the sound of Timorese pop music, two women — one of them the young woman who had just put on her new red folk dress — and two girls dance onstage with the painted image of the Timor mountains behind them. Joy and hope stand before the beautiful but cardboard landscape of East Timor.

Before that, the dance had been interrupted by a communal, political moment. It is a moment in which the film is undecided as to whether the images are documented or fictional, but clearly takes the stand of the Timorese, accompanying them in their plight. A man who appears to be a leader interrupts Bruce Springsteen's 'Dancing in the Dark' to announce that one of them is leaving Portugal for East Timor to fight the Indonesian occupant. Leaving for the guerrilla is a sort of dance in the darkness of war: 'Meus caros compatriotas: o Daniel vai estar mais perto de Timor. Vai estar a lutar' [My dear compatriots, Daniel is leaving to be closer to Timor. He will be fighting]. The speech continues, as the speaker urges those remaining on Portuguese soil to join the fight using whatever means can be used from afar: 'Mas nós cá fora também lutamos: temos outras armas, outros meios, outras formas de combater; nós lutamos contra a indiferença, lutamos contra o silêncio, contra o esquecimento, contra o espírito do deixa andar. Esta é a nossa forma de lutar, não nos esqueçamos disto, meus irmãos e minhas irmãs de Timor' [But we over here can struggle too: we have other weapons, other means, other forms of fighting; we fight against indifference, we fight against silence, against forgetfulness, against the spirit of leaving things as they are. This is our way of fighting, let's not forget this, my brothers, and my sisters of Timor]. The music that ensues is East Timorese folk accompanied by women dancing and preparing food in the kitchen, establishing a contrast with the idea of preparing to fight. All the while, and in agreement with the evil idea of fighting, the 'bad' Portuguese

---

[8] For a chronology (albeit incomplete, as the author himself recognizes) of events leading to the proclamation and international acknowledgement of East Timor as an independent, sovereign state, see A. Barbedo de Magalhães, 'Timor-Leste: tenacidade, abnegação e inteligência política', *Revista Camões*, 14 (2001), 26–39.

keeps drinking his *grappa*, feeding his sour soul, and getting ready to spark a fight. When a Timorese man accidently bumps into him and apologizes, saying he did not mean it, the Portuguese replies offensively — he is a topsy-turvy Caliban, the figure of the former colonizer now represented as the indigenous so often were deemed by the Europeans. An interlude song is heard over this scene (from 00:22:58 to 00:24:43): it is Peter Tosh's reggae theme 'Johnny B. Goode', lingering even after the shot changes towards the ballroom door — it is an intermediate theme, from a genre combining traits of Western pop culture with Afro beats which converged in Jamaican culture. But right afterwards, folk drums bring back Timorese resonances while women and men dance in folk attire, one of them (which suggests it is Daniel, the warrior-to-be) wearing traditional warrior costume. In the back, a rooster crows; the painted scenario is a permanent reminder of the mountains of Timor — a surrogate for the place where indeed the East Timorese guerrillas are hiding and fighting off, or getting ready to fight off, the Indonesians. Right after this, someone reads a message from Timor with the 'notícias amargas' [bitter news] of 'os filhos de Timor que caíram ontem pela nossa terra [the sons of Timor who fell for our land], and a long list follows, with names of men, younger and older, of their places of origin, of the children they are survived by, 'barbaramente assassinado[s] pelo ocupante' [barbarously assassinated by the occupant] (00:27:10). At this point, Margarida Gil's camera speaks through zooms and selective focus, indicating a language which associates the crescendo of war preparation with the names of the dead, to the head of the rooster in the cockfight, and finally to the face of the East Timorese folk dressed up to fight. Battle is always lurking underneath the festive atmosphere of the narrative; goodbyes and separation are the counterpart of love-making and the joy of living; sweet and bitter flowers sway in a permanent meditation on the dead. As is pronounced early in the film (see 00:07:48–00:07:53), 'Ninguém ri em Díli — ninguém ri em Lisboa' [Nobody laughs in Díli — nobody laughs in Lisbon].

Similarly to other works by this director, music is not taken as a mere presence in *Bitter Flowers*, but it acts as a relevant narrative element. Alongside the documental and symbolic role played by East Timorese folk songs and chants, and the contrast they are given by Western pop (in one of the boys' rooms the camera shows a poster of Elvis Presley), in *Bitter Flowers* one particular score underlines the artistic, fruitful, even beautiful connection between the East Timorese and the Portuguese, between former colonized and colonizer: the song 'Ai, Timor' composed by João Gil, brother of the director. In the film, it is performed by a choir of East Timorese children and young people, and the spectator perceives both the humming and the words in Tétum. The composition would afterwards acquire symbolic relevance when it became an anthem elegy for those who fell at Santa Cruz cemetery in 1991. In the lyrics written for that occasion by João Gil's group 'Trovante' outside the context of the film, a line stands out which points to the song itself as well as at the role the film played in reminding the Portuguese of this faraway, forsaken people: 'Se outros calam, cantemos nós' [If others are silent, let us sing]. *Bitter Flowers* echoes the beginning of this singing, the breaking of a long, unfair silence.

The film is clearly on the side of the East Timorese as it shows the urge of its refugees to go back and fight for independence. However, it does not romanticize or glorify the fight. In the scene before the death of Angelino, the boy comes into the room through the window and askes his brother if he is leaving. The answer is an affirmative nod, and Angelino verbalizes the brother's motives as he pleads to the brother to take him along: 'António, leva-me contigo' [António, take me with you]. But the brother gives Angelino a reality shock, telling him he is wrong in thinking he is a hero.

> Ouve, Angelino: tu talvez tenhas ficado com uma ideia errada sobre mim. Tu pensas que eu sou um herói. Um herói como nos filmes de cowboys. Mas não sou. A guerra não faz heróis. A guerra não distingue nada. Mata — mata tudo. Mata por bala. Mata por fome. Mata por doença. Que bom, Angelino — que sorte a tua, que não sabes o que é a guerra. Mas eu tinha a tua idade e fui apanhado por ela. [...] Não sabia o que era ter medo. Ter fome. Ver morrer os camaradas, a irmã, a mãe e o irmão pequenino.
> Se fosse agora, oferecias-te?
> Sim. Não sei. Agora já sei demais.
>
> [Listen, Angelino: maybe you've got a wrong idea about me. You think that I am a hero. A hero like in the cowboy films. But I'm not. War doesn't make heroes. It kills — kills everything. It kills with bullets. It kills with hunger. It kills with disease. You're lucky, Angelino — you're lucky you don't know what war is. But when I was your age I was taken by it. [...] I didn't know what it was to be afraid. To be hungry. To see my comrades die, my sister, my mother and my little brother.
> If it was now, would you volunteer?
> Yes. I don't know. Now I know too much.]

Actually, he says, he agreed to go to war because he had seen his family slaughtered but at present he no longer knows if he would, as war makes no heroes.

As António walks off the frame, the camera stands still. In the following scene his fiancée shows a gloomy face and looks away, her beautiful dark eyes receiving what little light is left and the rest of her features dimmed. António's silhouette passes in front of the scenario with the painted mountains and he leaves the frame at the right side as the camera zooms into the plywood landscape and a rooster's crow is heard announcing the dawn. A huge tree root and trunk in the early morning is the last shot and it seems to herald a new day.

East Timor is revisited in Margarida Gil's filmic work nine years after *Bitter Flowers* in *O Anjo da Guarda* [*Guardian Angel*] (1998). In this feature film, a fiction made for the big screen, the Asian territory serves as a backdrop for the Freudian tribulations of Luísa, a psychiatrist mourning the recent suicide of her father and going through her own midlife crisis. The dialogues of the film were written by the director and the writer Maria Velho da Costa. Timor is a faraway reference, the place where Luísa's father spent a relevant part of his life and one that he regrets not having shown her himself. After learning about her father's death, Luísa arrives home only to listen to his voice on the phone message recorder telling her how he would have wanted to point her a direction for living ('Gostaria de dizer-te "Vai para ali, para ali"' [I would like to tell you 'Go this way, that way']), or even to show her a free country ('gostaria de indicar-te um país livre'), which the spectator assumes is Timor, still occupied in 1998. The outcome of the father's wishes is annulled by his suicide; the outcome of the country's will to become a nation would take yet another four years.

Unable to retrieve or conjure up her father's presence, Luísa is left with his voice and with the film he shot in Timor, which she plays back alone in her apartment. Once more, the former colony is the realm of distance and longing — only this time as the irretrievable domain of a dead father, someone who represents the colonizer attempting to come to terms with his own existence (as colonizer?). The new Portugal which freed itself from a long dictatorship twenty-four years before the film premiered is somewhat like Luísa: reckoning the images of a former colony as the symbol of the loss of a father, grappling to keep a fragile emotional balance. In the film she eventually finds it in a relationship with a dying man who tends the roses in his garden: caring for one's private Eden offers a way to deal with one's traumatic past, the memory of which takes a long time to fade.

In the films of Margarida Gil, East Timor comes forth in a distanced, dislocated, disembodied image, inevitably through Western eyes. Whenever the living bodies of the East Timorese are indeed present and visible, as in *Bitter Flowers*, they dwell within an artificial, painted landscape. The refugee camp that shelters them and allows for their subsistence is ornamented with the illustration of the mountains but lacks the flame of the true communion with the land; rather, it is the people's longing to return to their island that sparks action. At the end of this television feature, when Angelino dies at the hands of the drunken Portuguese, the latter gets up and leaves, abandoning the lifeless boy. Another young man holds the dying boy, struggling to call his brother, and Angelino whispers when the latter arrives: 'Vais-te embora, não vais? Vai — eu vou logo ter contigo' [You are leaving, aren't you? Go — I will be joining you soon]. He then succumbs. The camera stands still as the brother walks off the frame, leaving Angelino behind: the body of Timor laid to rest in a foreign land, but its soul departed to the Asian island.

Otherwise, in *Guardian Angel*, the idea of the East Timorese people is transmitted through a voice (of someone unwillingly representing the former colonizer) coming from beyond the world of the living. It is an image of the people in the force of their soul and its manifestation; the image of a country on the verge of establishing itself as a free, independent nation, which founds its independence on cultural traditions and political will. These images may be conveyed verbally (through poetry and song lyrics, or in the voice of the dead father of *Guardian Angel*), through movement (the ritualistic dances), or in the visuality of the plywood landscape scenario. In *Bitter Flowers*, a film made (produced, directed, photographed, composed) by Portuguese but performed mostly by East Timorese, all these symbols, tokens of a soul, come forward to compose the full body of a country through its individuals. In Margarida Gil's TV film, the people of East Timor are characterized as a homogeneous and relatively tight-knit group who dwell away from home and revive the habits and traditions of the geographically distant homeland but seem to accept the welcoming linguistic environment they share with and within the post-colonial metropolis (albeit in its dismal outskirts). Among a sense of zeal for cultural heritage and complex layers of domination, the film establishes a primarily human geography, based on gazes and facial expressions, in which the work of music, of shot direction, of light and shade plays a fundamental role.

Adventures in Mozambique and the Portuguese Tendency to Forget: A Radical Critique of Portuguese Late Colonialism by Ângela Ferreira

Lurdes Macedo and Viviane Almeida[1]

CICANT[2] — Universidade Lusófona, Centro Universitário do Porto, and NETCult / CEHUM — Universidade do Minho

Introduction

This article aims to present a critical reflection on the way in which the film *Adventures in Mozambique and the Portuguese Tendency to Forget* (2015, 19'),[3] directed by Portuguese-Mozambican artist Ângela Ferreira (b. 1958),[4] and part of the Tate Modern collection in London, contrasts two realities experienced in Mozambique during the late colonial period. The first reality is that of the Portuguese settlers who, in an urban environment, enjoyed a modern lifestyle while perpetuating the construction of a historically extemporaneous empire. The second reality is that of the indigenous peoples who, in the remote territories, experienced the intrusion into their traditional way of life of an ethnology with obscure intentions. *Late colonial* refers to the period between 1945, which marked the beginning of a new post-WWII world order, and 1975, the year of Mozambique's independence.

To this end, the film under analysis, which won the Loop Fair Acquisition Award and is part of the Novo Banco Photo award-winning installation *A Tendency to Forget* (2015), presents a selection of images from the documentary *Mozambique: On the Other Side of Time* (1997, 58'),[5] intercut with images selected from *Margot Dias: Ethnographic Films, 1958–1961* (2016).[6] Ferreira's idealized composition of images constitutes the visual narrative that confronts the direct

---

[1] Ph.D. research grant from the Foundation for Science and Technology, I.P. (reference 2023.03741. BD).

[2] doi:10.54499/UIDB/05260/2020.

[3] *Adventures in Mozambique and the Portuguese Tendency to Forget*, dir. by Ângela Ferreira (2015). Hereafter referred to as *Adventures in Mozambique*.

[4] Professor at the Faculty of Fine Arts, University of Lisbon. Hereafter referred to as Ferreira.

[5] *Moçambique: no outro lado do tempo* (Beja filmes, 1996), '[on DVD]'. Hereafter referred to as *On the Other Side of Time*.

[6] *Margot Dias: filmes etnográficos, 1958–1961*, dir. by Margot Dias, org. by Catarina Alves Costa (Cinemateca, Museu Nacional de Etnologia, 2016), '[on DVD]'. Hereafter referred to as *Ethnographic Films*.

Portuguese Studies vol. 40 no. 2 (2024), doi:10.1353/port.00016, pp. 202–17

and, at the same time, intimate speech extracted from the diaries of Margot Dias (1908–2001) and the reports of the missions led by Jorge Dias (1907–1973), as ethnologists involved in the study of the Maconde of Mozambique (1957–61). It should be noted that the Dias couple were working for the *Missão de Estudos das Minorias Étnicas do Ultramar Português* [Mission for the Study of Ethnic Minorities in Portuguese Overseas Territories] (MEMEUP), sponsored by the *Ministro do Ultramar* [Ministry for Overseas Territories].[7] Although Margot was considered, until recently, a secondary figure in the missions, Ferreira gives her the same status as Jorge Dias in this work. In the same vein, Almeida, Zanete and Macedo show that Catarina Alves Costa's studies confirm that many of the works carried out during the missions were authored by Margot, in addition to the *Ethnographic Films*.[8]

On the Other Side of Time could be interpreted as a nostalgic manifesto from a generation of people of Portuguese origin who, having been born and/ or lived in Mozambique during late colonialism, remembered the former colony as the place where they 'lived the best years of their lives' (06'18"), a *Paradise Lost* to which it would be impossible to return. Despite the message in the documentary's opening note — 'To the current Mozambican homeland and its people, the producers sincerely wish that they consolidate their just independence in peace' (00'15"-00'45") — it is permeated by a discourse that validates the idea, problematized by authors such as Cunha, Macedo and Cabecinhas, of 'a predominantly mild colonialism, conducted by a people [...] free from racism or from exploitation practices'.[9]

The *Ethnographic Films* are a DVD collection that brings together the images and sound captured by Margot Dias during the missions to study the Maconde of Mozambique. Reorganized with careful editing by Catarina Alves Costa, these films reveal, in the words of Sanches, 'the desire to preserve and record Maconde culture at a time when it could still be recorded in its "purity"'.[10]

Even so, despite the rigorous work put into compiling and editing these films, it is essential to take into account Hall's observations when he argued that domination should be understood 'not only in terms of economic exploitation and physical coercion, but also in broader cultural or symbolic terms, including the power to represent someone or something in a certain way'.[11] It should be

[7] Hereafter referred to as MEMEUP.
[8] Viviane Almeida, Renata Flaiban Zanete and Lurdes Macedo, 'Autoria em Margot Dias pela lente revivescente da pós-memória', *Ex aequo*, 47 (2023), 117–36, doi:10.22355/exaequo.2023.47.0 9.
[9] Luís Cunha, Lurdes Macedo and Rosa Cabecinhas, 'Flows, Transits and (Dis)connection Points: Contributions towards a Critical Lusophony', *Comunicação e Sociedade*, 34 (2018), 165–82 (p. 170), doi:10.17231/comsoc.41(2022).3698.
[10] Manuela Ribeiro Sanches, 'Margot Dias: Filmes Etnográficos, 1958–1961', *Análise Social*, 224 (2017), 714–18 (p. 715), <http://www.scielo.mec.pt/scielo.php?script=sci_arttext&pid=S0003-25732017000300014&lng=pt&tlng=es> (all translations are our own, unless otherwise indicated).
[11] Stuart Hall, 'The Spectacle of the Other', in *Representation: Cultural Representations and Signifying Practices*, ed. by Stuart Hall, Jessica Evans and Sean Nixon (UK: Sage Publications, 2003), pp. 223–78 (p. 259).

noted that *A Tendency to Forget* — the installation that contains *Adventures in Mozambique* — is the result of a long process of research into the erasure of colonial memory and the refusal to make historical reparations, which became the theoretical basis for Ferreira's doctoral thesis, defended in 2016.[12] This *in situ* installation is made up of a large-scale sculptural structure, with an architecture reminiscent of the building of the former Ministry of Overseas Territories, whose stairs lead the viewer up into a small-scale auditorium where they can watch the film that is the subject of this study. The installation also includes a set of seven large-format photographs depicting the former Ministry of Overseas Territories building and the National Museum of Ethnology building, arranged outside the sculptural structure.

The hypothesis put forward to open this reflection is that *Adventures in Mozambique* constitutes a radical critique of the Portuguese colonial system in this territory in the 1950s, 1960s and 1970s, based on the renewed application of the artist's own concept of 'the return of the gaze' to the methodology of constructing the filmic object.

To support this hypothesis, it should first be noted that the research carried out by the Dias couple with the Maconde was part of the MEMEUP under the ideology of the colonial policy imposed by a fascist dictatorship. In this case, addressing the power relations between ethnologists in the service of the colonizer and the colonized Maconde on the Mueda Plateau — where Mozambique's liberation movements were beginning to emerge — inevitably brings colonial issues under the lens of the critique of 'post-post-colonialism', as enunciated by Ferreira.[13] Secondly, it is worth emphasizing that Ferreira's film is the result of a research process that questions the relationship between observing and being observed, especially when the observers are European ethnologists with a supposedly neutral gaze towards traditional African cultures. Ferreira's enquiry takes us from the panopticon to 'the return of the gaze'.

The panopticon, originally proposed by Jeremy Bentham and later developed by Michel Foucault, defines the dyad to 'see without being seen' or 'be seen without seeing', which, for the English philosopher at the end of the Enlightenment, took the form of a radial architecture capable of guaranteeing permanent surveillance of what went on inside prisons. Foucault recovered the concept, noting the versatility of its applications: 'it serves to reform prisoners, but also to treat patients, to instruct schoolchildren, to confine the insane, to supervise workers, to put beggars and idlers to work.'[14] Ironically, it was Foucault himself who had studied, in his earlier analysis, the 'pure reciprocity' of gazes that puts in tension the binarism that relates the power to observe

---

[12] Ângela Ferreira, 'Artistic Discourse as a Device for Innovation in the Discussion of Post-postcolonialism' (unpublished doctoral thesis, University of Lisbon, 2016).
[13] Ibid.
[14] Michel Foucault, *Discipline and Punish: The Birth of the Prison*, trans. by Alan Sheridan, 2nd edn (New York: Vintage, 1995), p. 205.

with the power to punish. In Velasquez's painting *Las meninas*, Foucault had noticed that 'subject and object, the spectator and the model, reverse their roles to infinity'.[15] Consequently, 'the return of the gaze' offers us the possibility of admitting the instability and bidirectionality of the dyad proposed by the panopticon.

Ferreira goes further, revisiting and renewing the concept of 'the return of the gaze' which, instead of centring on the possibility of reciprocity of gaze between the subjects of the dyad, instead focuses on the intentional act of using a camera to film those who filmed (or those who observed without being observed). In fact, Ferreira is clear about her proposal, acknowledging that she filmed the images used in *Adventures in Mozambique* while they were playing on a screen: 'There are two devices I use to underline my approach or my subtle observation, one by not using the original material — I filmed a television — and the other by pixelating faces and bodies.'[16] Thus, the way the artist approaches the concept allows her to place the viewer of *Adventures in Mozambique* in the position of *voyeur* of those who were once the *voyeurs*.

In other words, this article aims to understand how Ferreira, as a researcher and artist, by introducing her own approach to 'the return of the gaze' in the construction of *Adventures in Mozambique*, inaugurates a new way of bringing to light the unique and complex contradictions of late colonialism in Mozambique.

In order to test this hypothesis, we began by reviewing *Adventures in Mozambique*, then we reviewed the ethnographic films made by Margot Dias, and finally we watched *On the Other Side of Time* for the first time. The next step was to carry out a bibliographical survey capable of covering the essentials of the use of the filmic object in Ferreira's work, the ethnographic missions of the Dias couple and the structuring concepts, especially 'the return of the gaze', which support the hypothesis. Ferreira was also interviewed to better understand the creative process behind *Adventures in Mozambique*. Finally, we returned to this film for an analytical viewing and critical interpretation that would allow us to test the hypothesis and reflect on the results of the research. To support the research for this study, we also watched the film *Makwayela* (1977) by Jean Rouch and Jacques d'Arthuis.

It should be noted that this study is the result of an investigation, started in 2020, looking at the memory and representations of the Dias couple's work in Mozambique, based on the works of Catarina Alves Costa and Ângela Ferreira. This research, as a whole, also included a visit to the National Museum of Ethnology to appreciate the collection related to these ethnologists, as well as watching the interview given by Margot Dias to Catarina Alves Costa and

[15] Michel Foucault, *The Order of Things* (1966; London: Routledge, 1974), pp. 3–16, 4–5.
[16] Sérgio B. Gomes, 'Se depender de Ângela Ferreira, o legado colonial não vai ter sossego', <https://www.publico.pt/2015/10/02/culturaipsilon/noticia/se-depender-de-angela-ferreira-o-legado-colonial-nao-vai-ter-sossego-1709539> [accessed 20 December 2023].

Joaquim Pais de Brito (1996) and the documentaries *Viagem aos Makonde de Moçambique* (2019)[17] and *Margot* (2022)[18] by Catarina Alves Costa. This accumulated *corpus*, the subject of other publications, strengthens the research presented in this article.

In order to better contextualize this study, the proposed critical reflection will begin with a brief approach on the use of filmic objects in Ferreira's artistic career, then move on to analyse *Adventures in Mozambique* based on the research hypothesis and, finally, present some conclusions.

Considerations on the Filmic Object in the Work of Ângela Ferreira

Analysing Ferreira's artistic career emphasizes the constancy of the approach to the colonial past linking Portugal and Mozambique, as well as the constant presence of the filmic object in the artist's work, which mediates between the creator's intentions and the viewers' reception. In other words, in the conception of the work, the artist brings together different languages which, in a polyhedral way, organize different readings of a narrative. Without any intention of exhaustively analysing the use of film in Ferreira's work, it is worth mentioning some of the most significant examples. In *For Mozambique* (2008), a work in three series, the artist includes the filmic object in the structure/ sculpture made up of kiosks created by the Latvian-Russian artist Gustav Klucis in 1922, which evokes the optimism of the period following the Russian revolution in the 1920s. To do this, she uses extracts from the film *Makwayela*, shot in Mozambique by the French filmmaker and ethnographer Jean Rouch (1917–2004), in collaboration with Jacques d'Arthuis. The Makwayela is a dance that was born as a form of protest against the labour conditions of Mozambican workers in the mines of South Africa. In this film, workers from a bottle factory sing and dance in a post-independence Mozambique. In the words of one of the workers interviewed in the film, this revolutionary dance is a denunciation of situations of inequality and exploitation, creating a line of continuity between the colonial era and the post-independence present in the second half of the 1970s. According to Ferreira, the structure/sculpture that houses the films by Rouch and d'Arthuis is 'a manifestation of the atmosphere of utopian celebration in post-independence Mozambique', as well as 'a monument to the feelings of hope for the future of the country at that time'.[19] It should be noted that the moving image was recognized by the Mozambican government of the time as a powerful tool for consolidating a sense of belonging to the nation, which was still in its infancy. It was with this in mind that Rouch organized the *Super 8* workshops in the Mozambican capital and in rural areas of the country,

---

[17] *Viagem aos Makonde de Moçambique*, dir. by Catarina Alves Costa (Midas Filmes, 2019).
[18] *Margot*, dir. by Catarina Alves Costa (Midas Filmes, 2022).
[19] Ângela Ferreira, 'Each one teaches one', <https://angelaferreira.info/wp-content/uploads/51–74-angela-ferreira.pdf> [accessed 7 January 2024].

promoting cinema as one of the languages of emancipation.[20] It is worth noting that the third series of *For Mozambique*, dating from 2011 and entitled *Political Cameras*, includes two filmic objects, which are shown simultaneously from images related to the workshops conducted by Rouch at the Eduardo Mondlane University: the first, *The Workshops*, contains photographic documentation of the Jean Rouch *Super 8* film workshops; the second, *The Collective Films*, which contains two of the collaborative films that were produced during these workshops.

If, in *For Mozambique*, the filmic component recalled the first rehearsals of the country's independence as a moment of 'political utopia', through the lens of Jean Rouch, in a previous work, *Amnesia* (1997), the filmic object already revealed an incisive critique of the past that links Portugal to Mozambique, by progressively turning the camera's lens towards Portuguese colonialism and its consequences. This is a proposal in which this component plays a fundamental role in exercising the contradiction inherent in contemporary artistic processes. In this installation, in addition to the documentary film *On the Other Side of Time*, which plays on a loop on an old television set, other elements make up the imagery circuit with the aim of bringing viewers face to face with the amnesia of the colonial past. Oliveira characterizes the artist's work as a space in which the sculptural object, the text and the image, whether pictorial or filmic, recover the archive in ruins, thus stimulating 'a set of perceptions and sensations that cross time and are reconfigured in a critical way and with the potential to transform dogmas, thus opening up the field of the work of art.'[21] In this respect, the choice of the pieces that make up *Amnesia* is an invitation to reflect on the Portuguese colonial presence in Mozambique. If, on the one hand, the documentary establishes a vivid connection with pleasant memories of the colonial past through 'unforgettable images recorded somewhere on the other side of time' (06'20"), on the other, the other elements lead to questions of the exploitation of human and natural resources and the domination perpetrated by the Portuguese on the indigenous population of this former colony. Of particular note are the three statues of Ngungunhane, by the Portuguese ceramist Rafael Bordalo Pinheiro, representing the life of this legendary Vatua ruler who was captured and forcibly brought to captivity in Portugal, as well as the solid wooden chairs, a family heirloom of Ferreira's. Visually, the arrangement of the pieces contributes to this contradiction between narratives competing for the same space. In this regard, Leal identified the ability of many of Ferreira's works to establish connections with different events in Portugal's colonial past, in which the artist's memory and personal experience were implicated.[22] It is no wonder, then, that the experience of living

---

[20] Filipa Oliveira, 'The Tiger's Leap', in *Political Cameras: Ângela Ferreira* (Edinburgh: Stills Scotland's Centre for Photography, 2013), pp. 4–7 (p. 4).
[21] Márcia Oliveira, 'Considerações sobre o arquivo em práticas artísticas pós-coloniais: uma reflexão a partir da obra de Ângela Ferreira', *Revista Faces de Eva, FCSH-UNL* (2018), 107–14 (p. 111).
[22] Patrícia Leal, 'Framer Framed in "A Tendency to Forget"', *artciencia.com, revista de arte, ciência e*

in such fractious regimes as Portuguese colonialism in Africa and Apartheid tuned Ferreira's works to her personal trajectory. In this sense, Ferreira says in an interview about her first anthological exhibition, entitled 'Em Sítio Algum' [No Place at All], that *Amnesia* is born out of a duality of feelings. On the one hand, the artist reaffirms her doubts about the current narratives on relations between Portugal and Mozambique and, on the other, she reaffirms a certain revolt and the collective 'desire to forget certain events'.[23] These feelings are in stark contrast to the nostalgic character of the documentary *On the Other Side of Time* shown in *Amnesia*. By questioning this consensual and structural forgetting in Portuguese society, Ferreira creates a dialogue with Candau, an author who recognizes forgotten memory as a 'construction site' and not simply a 'field of ruins'.[24]

By confronting the memories of the past, mediated by the images compiled of life in Mozambique during the colonial period, viewers can feel implicated in the work. It is, therefore, worth highlighting the concept of the 'implicated subject' formulated by Michael Rothberg, those who 'occupy positions aligned with power and privilege without being themselves direct agents of harm.'[25] Motivated by apparently innocent acts, this subject plays significant roles in the production and perpetuation of inequality and violence. In agreement, Erll postulates that 'thinking with the implicated subject is an important way forward for the successful decolonization of cultural memory.'[26]

In fact, Ferreira is an artist who is increasingly involved in her actions and commitments, which implies the courage to revive uncomfortable memories and the forcefulness of unveiling old premises. It is along these lines that Ângela Ferreira's artistic itinerary can include the work *A Tendency to Forget*.

Regarding the artist's work, Oliveira emphasizes the transformative and courageous potential of her creations: 'More than penetrable structures and more than minimalistic architectures, they are sites of critical tension and of resistance: to the still persistent colonialist language; to the deployment of power; to the erasure of history and memory.'[27]

While in *Amnesia* the images taken from the documentary *On the Other Side of Time*, together with other elements of the installation, were already an incisive critique of the Portuguese colonial endeavour, it is in *A Tendency to Forget* that this intentional use of the filmic object as an instrument of denunciation becomes more forceful and authorial. This finding is related to our hypothesis,

comunicação, 20–21 (Feb. 2016 — May 2017).

[23] Vítor Almeida and Luís Armando Vaz, *Entre Nós: entrevista a Ângela Ferreira*, online video recording, <https://educast.fccn.pt/vod/clips/2rjcth6ui3/desktop.mp4?locale=pt> [accessed 9 January 2024].

[24] Joël Candau, *Memória e identidade* (São Paulo: Contexto, 2011), p. 217.

[25] Michael Rothberg, *The Implicated Subject: Beyond Victims and Perpetrators* (Stanford, CA: Stanford University Press, 2019), p. 1.

[26] Astrid Erll, 'Relational Dynamics: Transcultural Studies and Memory Studies', in *Transcultural Mobilities and Memories*, ed. by Mário Matos and Joanne Paisana (Braga: Edições Húmus, 2023), pp. 35–54 (p. 46).

[27] Oliveira, 'The Tiger's Leap', p. 7.

which considers that the inclusion of the concept of 'the return of the gaze' as central to the construction of the filmic object, artistically modified by Ferreira in *Adventures in Mozambique*, ensures this space of critical tension and resistance described by Oliveira. In fact, it is the artist herself who admits that, in *Amnesia*, because *On the Other Side of Time* was not authorially intervened, a space of manoeuvre was created that allowed certain viewers to rekindle their nostalgia for colonial times. But what Ferreira meant to tell her public, as she said in the interview, was this: 'You're forgetting what you did in Africa. You must sort this out, and then we'll move on.'[28] With the working methodology adopted in *Adventures in Mozambique*, Ferreira refuses to grant this room for manoeuvre, restoring its critical intention without deviation or hesitation.

This recovery of archived images in a 'field in the making' dialogues with the idea of a camera that positions itself for a political reading of the filmic object, placing it at the centre of contemporary debates. As such, Ferreira aims to question the current narrative fuelled by persistent vices in the way Portugal understands its colonial past. This is the dynamic that *A Tendency to Forget* aims to subvert.

Adventures in Mozambique: Dialogue among Various Archives for 'the return of the gaze'

Adventures in Mozambique should be understood from two points of view which, although distinct, are not mutually exclusive, but rather complement each other. On the one hand, it is evidence of continuity in Ferreira's career, with the inclusion of the filmic object in the work of art, with the recurrence of the theme of colonial memory, and with the intersection between political experience lived in the first person and aesthetic creation as an expression of that experience. It is worth remembering that Ferreira was born in Mozambique in 1958, growing up there during late colonialism, and also lived the first part of her adult life in South Africa during Apartheid. On the other hand, this film is evidence of the evolution to another level in this same trajectory, with the artist taking certain risks to make her message more forceful. Thus, at the same time that she takes the risk of extending the theme of colonial memory to historical reparations, she also takes the risk of a new approach to the filmic object, intervening for the first time in the original images (for example, by pixelating the bodies and faces) and, above all, incorporating her own concept of 'the return of the gaze' in the construction of her critique of the colonial system in Mozambique.

Naturally, this evolution should be understood in a broader sense, starting with *A Tendency to Forget*. According to the artist, the process of researching

---

[28] Viviane de Almeida, Lurdes Macedo and Renata Flaiban Zanete, 'A Tendency to Forget: Repairing (the) Past to Resist Forgetting. Interview with Artist Ângela Ferreira', *Vista*, 13 (2024), 1–22 (p. 16), doi:10.21814/vista.5524.

and designing this installation took five long years, which reveals a sense of density and depth that is becoming unusual in contemporary art. After more than two decades of a solitary and misunderstood journey,[29] Ferreira definitively inscribed the discussion about Portugal's colonial past in contemporary art with *A Tendency to Forget*.

Looking back at the reception and development of post-colonialism in Portugal, in its many guises, including artistic, Ribeiro noted that at the end of the 1990s, Ferreira presented disruptive works about Portugal's colonial past 'that left critics more or less mute. They were still "unclassifiable" works. It was still a time between mourning and trauma, silence and narrative crisis, a hesitant time like all beginnings, between a mythology and a lusotropical phraseology with deep roots in Portuguese society'.[30] For this very reason, the importance of Ferreira's work lay in the fact that it gave impetus to 'the beginning of a critical reflection on the Portuguese colonial past and its end, in a comparative and cosmopolitan dimension.'[31]

It is no surprise that *A Tendency to Forget* generated controversy at its launch and was the target of fierce criticism, especially from the Portuguese anthropology and ethnology community, as Ferreira acknowledges in the interview.[32] As Ribeiro recognizes, 'this is the tension that still characterizes Portuguese language, politics and criticism today'.[33] After winning the 2015 Novo Banco Photo Award, the installation began to attract increasing attention from the media and the public, including internationally. Soon afterwards, *Adventures in Mozambique* was acquired by Tate Modern and won the Loop Fair Acquisition Award. LOOP, founded in 2003, is an international platform dedicated to the study and promotion of the moving image in contemporary art discourses. It is in this way that the film under analysis achieves the recognition that brings to light its intrinsic value as a filmic object and, consequently, gives it autonomy as a work of art.

In fact, *Adventures in Mozambique* is the cathartic experience with which the viewer's visit to Ferreira's installation culminates (see Fig. 1), after appreciating the modernity and grandeur of the architecture of the two buildings that best symbolize Portuguese late colonialism, through the photos, and to enter 'the belly of the beast', i.e. the sculptural structure that represents them.

It is worth pointing out that this is an experience that could be understood as 'museum cinema',[34] which Parente and Carvalho refer to as being 'marked by the displacements it produces in relation to the hegemonic models that

---

[29] José Marmeleira, 'A descolonização continua', <https://www.publico.pt/2015/10/02/culturaipsilon/noticia/a-descolonizacao-continua-1709488> [accessed 8 January 2024].

[30] Margarida Calafate Ribeiro, 'Viagens no contemporâneo: pós-colonialismo, cosmopolitismo e programação', *Revista Mulemba*, 12.22 (2020), 127–47 (p. 132), doi:10.35520/mulemba.2020.v12n22a39821.

[31] Ibid.

[32] Almeida, Macedo and Zanete, '*A Tendency to Forget*', p. 8.

[33] Ribeiro, 'Viagens no contemporâneo', p. 132.

[34] André Parente and Victa de Carvalho, 'Entre cinema e arte contemporânea', *Revista Galáxia*, 17 (June 2009), 27–40 (p. 34).

FIG. 1. Detail view of the interior of the small-scale auditorium (with visitor watching the film). Source: angelaferreira.info

face them, seeking new ways of seeing and being'.[35] The authors go on to suggest that this 'museum cinema' is different not only because of the device, but also because of the strategies that create new subjectivations. This is how this type of filmic object comes about: in the disjunction between recognition and displacement, in a 'creative game of relationships between spectators and devices'.[36]

In this sense, the challenge that *Adventures in Mozambique* poses to its viewers is to reframe late colonialism in Mozambique, departing from the ethnologist couple Margot and Jorge Dias's experience, based on four archive recordings that Ferreira skilfully combines in the same device to create a filmic object embodied in the concept of 'the return of the gaze': images selected from *On the Other Side of Time* that confront Margot Dias's confessions in her diaries; and images selected from *Ethnographic Films* that confront Jorge Dias's confidential reports to MEMEUP. It is in this contradiction, between images and audio, between the senses of sight and hearing, that the artist's originality and intentional denunciation of a forgotten colonial order lie.

The film begins with images taken from *On the Other Side of Time*, of the then city of Lourenço Marques,[37] now Maputo, which show its European urban matrix. The modern avenues, lined with imposing buildings, overflow with elegant cars and people with a happy, relaxed air. The movement denoting the daily life of a vibrant and cosmopolitan society will, later on, contrast with the

---

[35] André Parente and Victa de Carvalho, 'Entre cinema e arte contemporânea', p. 38.
[36] Ibid.
[37] Hereafter referred to as LM.

images of the community life of the Maconde in northern Mozambique. At the same time, a narrator who speaks in Portuguese with a German accent, suggesting that it is the voice of Margot Dias, begins to describe the departure for the first study mission of the Maconde of Mozambique, on 16 July 1957. It is at the stopover in Nigeria that Margot sees herself 'for the first time among blacks only' (00'49"), while the images show the streets of LM populated with white people. She remarks that 'the enormous variety of types is surprising. The faces and formats are very different' (00'54"). While she talks about the physical (and possibly also psychological) differences that characterize black people, the images selected by Ferreira reveal a variety of medium shots and close-ups of the faces of the city's white inhabitants.

This dissertation is immediately followed by images of places in nature and of the Maconde living their slow daily lives in the villages of the Mueda Plateau, selected from *Ethnographic Films*. Accompanying them is the voice of a narrator who, in the guise of Jorge Dias, confesses the obscure political intentions behind the ethnographic study missions. In the 1957 report, he mentions that the Minister of Overseas Territories had asked him to gather information on what was happening politically and socially in the territories neighbouring the Mueda Plateau, specifically Rhodesia and Niassa, and to visit them if possible. In the 1959 campaign report, Jorge Dias says: 'Although we are not politicians, and we are reluctant to venture into domains unrelated to our professional interests, we are required to do so, given the close relationship between the political and the social' (03'08"–03'24"). This passage ends with Jorge Dias assuming that the information he has gathered in the field, due to its explosive content, cannot be made public.

The first two sequences of *Adventures in Mozambique* set the tone and rhythm for what will be seen throughout the film. In a succession of sequences interspersed between narrations by Margot and Jorge Dias, we can see, in each of them, the confrontation that operationalizes Rancière's idea of 'establishing a radical opposition between two kinds of representation, the visible image and the account through the word, and two kinds of certification, proof and testimony.'[38] However, more than the opposition between the two kinds of representation, Ferreira radically opposes the explicit content of images and words, seeking to uncover what is really going on, beyond the obvious appearances.

Thus, Margot Dias's accounts of her experience with the Maconde are illustrated, always in a counterpoint, with images of the life of the settlers. When she refers to the difficulty of photographing the Maconde, the image that appears on screen is of a single black man in a group of whites socializing on a terrace. When she reports that young Maconde women cover themselves with cloths to escape her camera, the images shown are of young white women in bikinis on the lively beaches of LM. In contrast, and as a way of guaranteeing

---

[38] Jacques Rancière, *O espectador emancipado* (Lisbon: Orfeu Negro, 2010), p. 134.

> When the child was brought to her,
> it was already dead and smelled rotten.

FIG. 2. Ângela Ferreira, *Adventures in Mozambique and the Portuguese Tendency to Forget*, 2015 | Video Still

the privacy that was not negotiated in the original filming conducted by Margot Dias, Ferreira pixelates the faces portrayed in *Ethnographic Films*.

While Margot tells us the terrible story of a Maconde woman who, after a week with her dead foetus stuck in her pelvis, is taken to Mocímboa da Praia where the Portuguese doctor refuses to treat her immediately and she too ends up dying, the viewer is confronted with images of white settlers having fun at parties and nightclubs (see Fig. 2). This contrast based on provocation and denunciation reaches its climax at 08'53" when, together with the image above, in which a white couple dance carelessly, we hear what is transcribed in the English subtitles.

This impactful account prompts Margot to reflect in the form of a question — 'How can black people, who are really so caring towards children and the sick, have respect for white people?' (09'16"–09'25") — while the images show young white dancers during a cabaret performance, focusing on close-ups of their hips.

The description of the persecution, imprisonment, and murder, for political reasons, of several Maconde people with whom Margot lived, is accompanied by images of settlers enjoying themselves in swimming pools and luxury clubs. Finally, the last remark, in which Margot recounts her last visit to the village of Nkumi where she was received with indifference, and her interpreter was questioned by the locals in order to find out if Margot and Jorge Dias were spies, is accompanied by images of the then city of Porto Amélia, now Pemba, much more modest than LM, but closer to the Maconde Plateau. It is in this final sequence that Margot concludes that it will not be possible to return to the Mueda Plateau.

In turn, Jorge Dias's narrations, which reveal confidential information about the political situation in northern Mozambique and cross-border areas, are illustrated, also in a counterpoint manner, with images documenting the most traditional aspects of Maconde culture identified in his ethnographic studies. While advising that the return of 'indigenous Portuguese' immigrants from Tanganyika should be avoided, in order to contain the spread of subversive ideas among the Maconde of the Plateau, the viewer is shown images of male initiation rituals, traditional to their culture. At the same time as he talks about the concern felt by the people because one of their sovereigns is imprisoned in LM, the images we are shown depict the Maconde in healthy coexistence. When he advises that there should be a difference in treatment 'between an educated negro and a primitive one' (15'09"–15'15"), as well as good relations with the former, because he is the only one capable of influencing the people, the images on screen show the unity among the Maconde during their festivities.

It is in this opposition of opposites that Ferreira finds what she was looking for in the creative process for *Adventures in Mozambique*. As she said in an interview: 'I wanted to find something that was [...] as if the camera had turned against them [the Dias couple].'[39] It should be noted that, in the composition that results in this filmic object, the artist problematizes the 'pure reciprocity' of gazes that establishes the possibility of bidirectionality in the dyad proposed by the panopticon. In order to understand this problematization, it is worth returning to Amad's considerations on 'the return of the gaze' as a contribution of post-colonial theories to film studies. The author recalls that ethnographic films were produced under a colonial and racist ideology while also proposing that a radical difference must be admitted in the spectator–screen relationship in old non-fiction films compared to classic fiction films, which appeal to 'an invisible-eye model' of spectatorship. Finally, Amad clarifies that old non-fiction films are the subject of discussion about 'the return of the gaze' because they 'abound with evidence of the camera being acknowledged by the subjects filmed.'[40]

In *Adventures in Mozambique*, by pixelating the faces of the Maconde captured by the lens of Margot Dias's camera, Ferreira not only seeks to restore dignity to the subjects filmed, as a form of historical reparation, but also avoids any misunderstanding as to her approach to the concept of 'the return of the gaze'. Without evidence of the subjects recognizing the camera, their gaze is not returned to the viewer. Thus, by using images captured from a television screen, the artist proposes another return of the gaze, transferred from the filmed subject to the camera and to the viewer themselves. It is in this renewal of the concept of 'the return of the gaze', as well as in its application to the creative process, that Ferreira interweaves a series of new possibilities. Firstly,

---

[39] Almeida, Macedo and Zanete, 'A Tendency to Forget', p. 13.
[40] Paula Amad, 'Visual Riposte: Looking Back at the Return of the Gaze as Postcolonial Theory's Gift to Film Studies', *Cinema Journal*, 52.3 (2013), 49–74 (p. 51).

she offers herself the chance to turn the camera against Margot and Jorge Dias, as she has so incessantly desired to do, exposing the contradictions of the work they carried out with the Maconde in Mozambique. With her camera, which is undoubtedly political in its approach, Ferreira shows that, as well as carrying out ethnographic studies of a scientific nature, the objectives of the Dias couple's missions also involved spying on the political situation in northern Mozambique, at a time when liberation movements were beginning to emerge there.

Indeed, in *Adventures in Mozambique*, the viewer is confronted with this evidence, above all through the contradiction between the images they observe, which document the ethnographic study of Maconde community life, and the accounts of a narrator who wears the skin of Jorge Dias, revealing the obscure intentions of observing (without being observed) the possibly subversive relations of the Maconde with the neighbouring territories of Rhodesia, Niassa and Tanganyika. It should be noted that these reports show not only his observation of the context, but also the guidelines on how to proceed in that territory that he gave to MEMEUP.

Secondly, with this renewal of 'the return of the gaze', Ferreira offers viewers the chance to immerse themselves in the 'belly of the beast' and internalize the contrast between the life of the settlers and the life of the Maconde, as well as the ambiguity that permeated the work of Margot and Jorge Dias through the viewing of *Adventures in Mozambique*. In this way, the artist invites the viewer to become involved in the creative process itself, since it is completed through the tacit agreement between the creation and reception of the work. It should be emphasized that the artist's intention is to allow the viewer to assume the role of voyeur behind the scenes of the missions undertaken by the Dias couple. In this case, the viewer has the possibility of becoming an 'implicated subject' in the sense of 'understanding how people can become "folded into" histories of injustice'.[41]

Finally, with this approach, and through the freedom of expression and creativity that characterize her, Ferreira obstructs the room for manoeuvre that had caused her discomfort in *Amnesia*, offering herself the possibility of finally saying what she wanted to say. Based on two film recordings that differ in what they bring to light — although they were made in the same place at the same time — the artist finally materializes her radical critique of the contradictions, singularities and complexities of late colonialism in Mozambique

The possibilities listed, offered by Ferreira's renewed approach to 'the return of the gaze', as well as its application to the construction of the filmic object, are evidence of Oliveira's postulate about the artist: 'Ferreira cannot be labelled as an artist who works in the ethnographic field, but certainly as an artist who challenges and subverts the traditional ethnographic and anthropological approach to materials, experiences and spectacle.'[42]

---

[41] Astrid Erll, 'Relational Dynamics: Transcultural Studies and Memory Studies', p. 46.
[42] Oliveira, 'The Tiger's Leap', p. 7.

Final Notes: The Three New Possibilities Based on the Renewal of 'the return of the gaze' by Ângela Ferreira

With the study described in this article, we sought to understand how, through the renewal of the concept of 'the return of the gaze' applied to the construction of the filmic object, Ferreira proposes her radical critique of the contradictions of late colonialism in Mozambique, solidifying this experience in *Adventures in Mozambique and the Portuguese Tendency to Forget*.

The choice of the word 'Adventures' in the title of the film seems to be intentional, not only because of what its supposed meanings reveal, but also because of the dialogue it establishes with the work. As an action that involves risk and whose outcome is uncertain, the word refers to the dual objectives of the Dias couple's ethnographic missions, and also, in a broader sense, to the contradictions of the Portuguese colonial endeavour. It should be noted that, in the title of the film, adventure is followed by oblivion. In fact, it is no coincidence that, in the first sequence of the documentary, the title of the installation that includes this filmic object, *A Tendency to Forget*, appears with a minimalist framing as a statement that emphasizes the attitude rooted in Portuguese society: the tendency to forget the darker side of its colonial past. With the development of the film narrative, Ferreira goes further, questioning the most conventional and established structures of thought by demonstrating a hitherto obliterated reality that the artist denounces in her work. In this way, *Adventures in Mozambique* subsidizes Leal's thinking when she states that 'The works by Ângela Ferreira [...] enable us to see how colonial matters in Portugal are still animated by amnesia and nostalgia'.[43]

After situating *Adventures in Mozambique* in a line of continuity that characterizes the artist's career — the theme of colonial memory, the inclusion of the filmic object in the work of art, and the intersection between political experience and aesthetic expression — the evolution that *Adventures in Mozambique* constitutes in this same trajectory was highlighted, with the extension of the theme of colonial memory to historical reparations, and above all with the incorporation of her renewed 'return of the gaze' in the construction of the filmic object. It should be remembered that this renewal of the concept allowed Ferreira to transfer 'the return of the gaze' from the filmed subjects to the camera and the viewer, while at the same time risking an authorial intervention in pre-existing images in conjunction with texts researched in archives.

As the analysis of *Adventures in Mozambique* shows, this development opened up three new possibilities for Ferreira. Firstly, the creative possibility of turning the camera on the Dias couple, who had filmed the Maconde during the missions' ethnographic films that they starred in. This is the return of the camera's gaze. Secondly, the relational possibility of involving the viewer in

---

[43]   Patrícia Leal, 'Framer Framed in "A Tendency to Forget"', p. 12.

the act of completing the work with the return of their gaze, by placing them as a voyeur behind the scenes of Margot and Jorge Dias's missions. This is the spectator's return of the gaze. Thirdly, the communicational possibility, through the application of the renewed concept it proposes to the construction of the filmic object, of bringing together the radical critique of late Portuguese colonialism in Mozambique into a dynamic totality. This dynamic totality expands with the contextualization of *Adventures in Mozambique* in the installation *A Tendency to Forget*, not only from the point of view of the expression of the artist's critical message, but also from the point of view of the spectator's experience of reception when viewing this filmic object in the 'belly of the beast' of late Portuguese colonialism that the building of the former Ministry of Overseas Territories symbolizes. In fact, this communicational possibility is validated by Ferreira when, in an interview, she states that, contrary to what she has done with her other works, she does not intend to revisit *A Tendency to Forget* because in it she said exactly what she wanted to say.[44]

It is by opening up these new possibilities, achieved through her own approach to the concept of 'the return of the gaze' applied to the construction of the filmic object, as well as by taking the risks she associated with it — in terms of theme, experimentation and methodology — that Ferreira expresses her denunciation of a colonial order that until then had not been revealed. Thus, with this filmic object which, in the words of the artist herself, 'wasn't just a film of grief or sadness, it was a film that caused some violent emotion',[45] Ferreira inaugurates a new approach to the contradictions that express the singularities and complexities of Portuguese colonialism in Mozambique, at a time when new African nations had already secured, or were one step away from securing, their independence. This approach is all the more inaugural if we accept Brás's idea of a paradigm in which 'colonial ambivalence continues to permeate contemporary cultural discourses and artistic practices, even when such practices and discourses appear to articulate a post-colonial critique'.[46] Reducing the room for manoeuvre for ambivalent interpretations, with which Ferreira challenges us in *Adventures in Mozambique*, demonstrates this originality in a proposal that breaks with the current paradigm.

---

[44] Almeida, Macedo and Zanete, 'A Tendency to Forget', p. 16.
[45] Ferreira in interview with the authors, on 19 November 2020.
[46] Patrícia Sequeira Brás, 'A ambivalência colonial nas imagens em movimento contemporâneas: o caso português', *Comunicação e sociedade*, 41 (2022), 91–103 (p. 98), doi:10.17231/comsoc.41(2022).3698.

How Bollywood Lost its Goan Rhythm:
An Interview with Bardroy Barretto,
Director of *Nachom-ia Kumpasar*

R. Benedito Ferrão

William & Mary, Virginia

Bardroy Barretto is the writer and director of the Konkani-language film, *Nachom-ia Kumpasar* (2014). He began his career in media in the 1980s and, from then, worked as an editor and also in advertising in the city of Bombay. *Nachom-ia Kumpasar* is his first full-length motion picture. Set in Goa and Bombay of the 1960s and inspired by real-life Goan entertainers, Barretto's film fictionalizes the period by portraying the lives of musicians from the era. The film demonstrates how Goan music, with its Portuguese influences, created the soundtrack for Bollywood in the second half of the twentieth century, while bearing witness to the part played by the Indian film industry, and film history, in undermining the legacy of Goan musicians. In this interview Barretto provides his perspective on how Bombay became a site of possibility for Goans at the end of Portuguese colonialism, their forays into entertainment giving rise to Goan, Konkani-language theatre (*tiatr*) and film, as well. Further, as *Nachom-ia Kumpasar* and its director evidence, Goan musicians not only brought their Portuguese colonial-era musical training to Bollywood, but also the rhythms of jazz. While such musical histories may be forgotten, and as Barretto's film and this interview make clear, the mark Goans left on Indian cinema's soundscape cannot fail to be heard.

This interview with the director was conducted over email in 2022.

* * * * *

RBF: What drew you to make this film and why choose the medium of a fictional feature rather than a documentary to chronicle the history of Goan musicians in Indian cinema?

BB: To start with, I had no idea that Goan musicians populated military/services/railways and circus bands and played the piano scores in sync with the films during the silent era. They entertained the elites in the jazz clubs in Bombay, Calcutta, Delhi, Bangalore, and even far away Burma (now Myanmar). They also played in the princely states' in-house bands. There were thousands of Goan musicians employed in British India.

Portuguese Studies vol. 40 no. 2 (2024), doi:10.1353/port.00017, pp. 218–28
© Modern Humanities Research Association 2024

FIG. 1. Still from *Nachom-ia Kumpasar* (2014) by Bardroy Barretto

Post-Independence, Prohibition was declared in the Bombay State (Bombay Prohibition Act 1949), which dealt a death blow to the jazz clubs, so these musicians gravitated toward the nascent Indian film industry and went on to change its soundscape. I discovered these musicians while doing research for *Nachom-ia Kumpasar*.

Goa did not have a film culture, save for a few films in the mid-1960s to 1970s. As a result, there was significantly less moving image documentation of Goa. So, when I set out to do *Nachom-ia Kumpasar*, a fictional feature was a natural choice as it is a popular mass medium versus a documentary. The idea was also to start a Konkani cinema movement and make Konkani cool as the younger population was shying away from it. Looking back, I think we did succeed, as just two films were released in 2014, and the number jumped to multiples of tens in the following years. Seeing the film's commercial success, many filmmakers joined the bandwagon to make more Konkani films.

Anthony Gonsalves (1927–2012) is one musician who stood out for me. I had the opportunity to talk to him and understand the world he came from. He is the one who orchestrated and harmonized Indian ragas, a form that is otherwise played in monotone. This blend of Western and Indian idioms changed the soundscape of Indian film music. I deliberated for a long time about doing a documentary on him but handed over my research to another filmmaker to do the documentary and to Naresh Fernandes for his book *Taj Mahal Foxtrot: The Story of Bombay's Jazz Age*.[1]

I had written a blog post on Gonsalves way back in 2010.[2] This is my only written material on the subject in the public domain.

---

[1] Naresh Fernandes, *Taj Mahal Foxtrot: The Story of Bombay's Jazz Age* (New Delhi: Lustre Press, 2012).
[2] Bardroy Barretto, 'Anthony Prabhu Gonsalves: A Profile', in *bardsworld* <https://bardroybarretto. blogspot.com/2010/11/anthony-prabhu-gonsalves-profile.html> [accessed 1 December 2022].

RBF: Before getting into the action, *Nachom-ia Kumpasar* begins with a voiceover that informs viewers of its belief that, for Goa, its story is its music. That music is identified in this opening moment as being a blend of Dravidian and Portuguese rhythms.

Adding to this idea, in *Taj Mahal Foxtrot: The Story of Bombay's Jazz Age*, Naresh Fernandes explains that while the Portuguese, who colonized Goa between 1510 and 1961, 'neglected higher education' in the region, the one thing they did attend to by 1545 was the establishment of 'parochial schools that put into place a solid system of musical training'.[3] In turn, this allowed Goans to function 'as the musicians of the [British Indian] Raj', because of their education in Western music.[4] As the hold of the feudal agricultural economy in Portuguese India decreased and jobs became scarcer, British India beckoned to Goans, and musical entertainment became a service they could provide there and then elsewhere in the British Empire, British Africa included.

Yet, as your film underscores so gracefully, Goans made 'Western' music their own. Is it true to say that while Goan music has marked Portuguese influences, Goan musicians always put a local spin on European music (even during the colonial era)? And/or is it also the case, as one sees in *Nachom-ia Kumpasar*, that Goans incorporated the inspirations they encountered as travellers beyond the shores of their homeland?

BB: When the Portuguese colonized the land of Goa and its people, they also inherited a social structure, that is the caste system, which was prevalent at that time. The *bamonns* (Brahmins) and the *chardos* (Kshatriyas) owned land and were at the top of this caste hierarchy. At the bottom were the *sudirs* (Shudras/Dravidians), who practised traditional occupations, artisans, and there were also the tribal or indigenous communities.

This lower stratum had its own traditional ritualistic rhyme and rhythm comprising drums, vocals, and sometimes cymbals, music which was passed down the generations orally and in practice. The tribal communities had rhythm in their blood. But it was the formal training in the parochial schools under Portuguese rule that got those at the lower end of society ready when British India beckoned. Now they could read and write music and amalgamate it into any musical composition and movement.

Being from the oppressed class, they also used music as a tool for social change, which gave rise to the popular form of Konkani music, simply called *cantaram* [songs], which bear Portuguese influence. The Western influence they encountered as music hands in British India was further fused into their own indigenous tribal rhythms. They wrote political protest songs about social evils such as dowry, land rights, alcoholism, and so on, which were prevalent at that time. They also wrote about love and affairs back home. They explored a range of topics and emotions in their music.

---

[3] Fernandes, *Taj Mahal Foxtrot*, p. 56.
[4] Ibid., pp. 56–57.

At the same time, the elites and the seminary-educated musicians mostly stuck to refined forms of music, namely the *mando*, *dulpod*, and devotional songs (usually hymns).

The film's voiceover articulates all this only as an observation. The visual with the voiceover is of a church with a *mestre* walking toward it, followed by a child holding a trumpet while his father and two musicians happen to stroll by. This vignette is imagined as occurring during the period of Portuguese India. The voiceover, along with the visual, is open to interpretation.

As another observation, if we superimpose the evolution of Goan music with that of Brazil, another former Portuguese colony, similar patterns will likely be observed. I spent a month in Brazil in 2007. The Afro-Portuguese blend gave rise to *forró* in Manaus, *frevo* in Recife, *axé* in Salvador de Bahia, and the smooth *samba* down south in Rio de Janeiro. I suppose this, too, is possible because of the Portuguese system of musical training which blended with African rhythms.

RBF: Inasmuch as *Nachom-ia Kumpasar* is a film about music in the Golden Era of the Indian film industry (late 1940s to 1960s), it is also a story about post-Portuguese Goa, beginning as the film does in Bombay in 1964. In a sense, this ties together the post-European trajectories of these regions which were, actually, both under Portuguese rule at some point in their histories. Through scenes set in *kudds*, the community halls Goans established for themselves in Bombay, and the shows that the characters Donna, Lawry, and their band play in that city, your movie acknowledges the deep links Goans have with Bombay. Furthermore, *Nachom-ia Kumpasar* considers how Goans contributed to the making of modern Bombay, as have so many communities in that cosmopolitan metropolis.

As your film looks back on the 1960s, how does it acknowledge the difference of that moment and what it made possible in Indian history? What lessons might we still learn from that time? And how different is that period in comparison to the contemporary moment?

BB: The large-scale emigration of Goans (cooks and musicians) to British India-ruled Bombay started after the Anglo-Portuguese Treaty of 1878.

Contrary to the popular notion that Goans mainly worked as cooks, seamen, and musicians, there was an immense contribution by Goans in varied other fields, be it medicine, the arts, literature, administration, education, advertising, journalism, and sports. This influence lasted till the early 1990s and played a large part in the making of modern Bombay. Sadly, their contribution is now reduced to small print or slowly being erased.

I landed in Bombay in 1988, three years before the liberalization of the Indian economy in 1991. Getting rid of the old to build anew was not so rampant; I could keenly observe the Goan community in Greater Bombay, which helped me re-construct (for the film) the *kudds*, the community halls, and the one-

FIG. 2. *Tiatr* performance in *Nachom-ia Kumpasar* (2014) by Bardroy Barretto

room-kitchen tenements in which they resided. The jazz clubs had disappeared, making way for Indian Orchestra Bars, and then, soon, Bombay changed to Mumbai in 1995. The Goans are now slowly dispersing to the distant suburbs for more extensive and affordable housing.

RBF: In addition to its use of Goan music, *Nachom-ia Kumpasar* is also mindful of other forms of Goan cultural production, including *tiatr* (which is scripted in Romi Konkani, is musical in style, and often addresses contemporary social and political issues). Again, this is a Goan art form that owes its history to Bombay, the first *tiatr*, Lucazinho Ribeiro's *Italian Bhurgo* [*Italian Boy*], having been performed there in 1892.[5]

Not only does Prince Jacob, a legendary actor of the Konkani stage, make an appearance in the film (and I will return to Pisso Santan, the character he plays, shortly), but the film's closing credits also feature a scene that is straight out of a *tiatr*. This musical scene includes a comedic performance by, among other actors, Prince Jacob and Donna, now playing roles as *tiatrists* as the film ends. In this interplay between stage and screen, music is the most obvious intermedial connection. How did *tiatr*, an often undervalued Konkani theatrical and literary art form, influence your making of this film?

BB: All the *tiatr* productions were based in Bombay till the late 1970s. They had their first few shows in Bombay and then travelled to Goa. Goa had *khells*, which are usually plays in three acts, that were staged during Carnival time and were performed in the open. In the 1970s, Rosario Rodrigues and, later, Rose Ferns were the pioneers to take these *khells* onto a stage, thus giving birth to *khell-tiatr*. Both these forms (*tiatr* and *khell-tiatr*) evolved and merged and are now simply called *tiatrs*.

Similarly, all the earlier Konkani films were helmed and produced by these same *Bombaimcars* (Bombay Goans). Their exposure to working in the growing

---

5   Fernandes, *Taj Mahal Foxtrot*, p. 53.

Indian film industry as musicians, film studio hands, and in film production gave them a head-start in cinema. Al Jerry Braganza (Antonio Lawrence Jerry Braganza) produced the first film in Konkani, *Mogacho Anvddo* [*Love's Craving*] in 1950 during Portuguese rule. For the second Konkani film, Goa had to wait for thirteen years. *Amchem Noxib* [*Our Luck*] was released in 1963, two years after Portuguese rule ended, and was produced by Frank Fernand, a noted film arranger then. He followed it up with *Nirmon* [*Destiny*] in 1966. Chris Perry joined in producing *Bhuierantlo Munis* [*Man from the Cave*] in 1977.

Save for a few Konkani films, most of the Konkani music was written for *tiatrs*. Both these forms, *tiatr* and Konkani films, owe their history to Bombay as the Bombay Goans (who played in the jazz clubs and film studios) are the pioneers of these art forms. If not for *tiatrs*, just producing Konkani music would not be commercially viable. These *tiatrists* and filmmakers had the wisdom to record these songs for posterity; I don't think they were paid any royalties.

All this changed with the advent of audio cassettes in the early 1980s; the production and marketing costs were not so prohibitive. Now, they could produce and monetize their music by selling cassettes. Local music labels, too, sprouted up in Goa.

All the songs that appear in my film were originally written by Chris Perry for his two musical shows, *Nouro Mhozo Deunchar* [*My Husband, the Devil*] and *Tum ani Hanv* [*You and Me*]. Chris Perry put Lorna through her paces for over six months in Bombay, rehearsing with his band; finally, she made her debut at Trincas in Calcutta and then played at Astoria in Bombay. A few years later, *Nouro Mhozo Deunchar* was Goa's introduction to Lorna. For the first time in the history of *tiatrs*, the band, which usually played from the pit, took centre stage. For the film, it was apt to migrate some songs to a *tiatr* setting as that is the medium the songs were written for.

RBF: When Donna first meets Lawry and his band in Bombay, he asks her to sing the song 'Pisso' [Madman] during a rehearsal. She suggests that despite its despondent theme, the song could be performed in a more upbeat fashion. Lawry finally relents and Donna's cheery spin on the song makes it a hit. Later in the film, when Lawry and Donna's relationship becomes irreparable, Donna declares that the only thing she will ever be married to is music.

What is compellingly portrayed here is her agency as a woman who not only has an impact on the band's sound but also expresses her creative ambition and self-belief apart from her professional and romantic relationships.

Could I ask you to comment on how much this drew from the history of that moment? I ask this especially given that the music in the film, much of it by Chris Perry (1928–2002) and Lorna Cordeiro (b. 1944), including 'Nachom-ia Kumpasar' [Let's Dance to the Rhythm] from which the movie derives its title, is actually from the period of its setting.

FIG. 3. Donna (Palomi Ghosh) sings in *Nachom-ia Kumpasar* (2014)
by Bardroy Barretto

BB: There was a story in the songs. The songs were set to a playlist to tell a story; later, the scenes were written to take the songs forward.

The main events in the film start in Bombay in 1964, just when Prohibition was lifted, and end in 1975 when the entertainment tax was raised for hotels and clubs playing western music, forcing these jazz and big band musicians towards making music for the Hindi film industry. The love story of Donna and Lawry is set within this timeline. Then, twenty years later, in 1995, when Bombay changed to Mumbai, Donna makes her comeback.

The song 'Nachom-ia Kumpasar' represents the spirit of a young Donna who just wants to sing and have a good time. The upbeat version of the theme keeps recurring whenever Donna wants to break free and turns blue when she's down.

For 'Pisso', the lyrics and music are diametrically opposed in terms of emotions. It is the sheer genius of Chris Perry to have set such an upbeat rhythm to a despondent theme. So, we started with a slightly morose version and used the original as Donna's take, thereby transforming how the band played the song.

All the songs are interpreted to tell a story; sometimes, the lines between their professional and real lives blur, but the characters' emotions ride on from one song to the next.

RBF: I would also like to ask you to reflect on *Nachom-ia Kumpasar*'s treatment of gender more generally. Two examples come to mind. Firstly, although Lorna Cordeiro is often described as 'The Nightingale of Goa', it is notable that her crooning style is not typically feminine; similarly, Donna sings in a manner that veers between being demure and, then, far from it. This is especially stark in the context of the rest of the band-members being men. What does this say about how women may have used the space of performance to craft their identities at this mid-century moment?

Then, in several scenes, news of goings-on in Bombay are made known in Goa through the appearance of a 'chorus' of three men who hang out by the village gathering spot, a large cross. Interestingly, these village gossips are men, their commentary on the characters' lives in Bombay and Goa ranging from such topics as the musicians' love affairs and failures and successes. As women are so often characterized as being gossips, was it a deliberate choice to have these characters be men? In your film (and elsewhere), what is the role of gossip itself as a form of community storytelling and information-sharing?

BB: Though the audiences in these clubs were the elites of South Bombay, the prodigious musicians who entertained them came from humble and strict Catholic upbringings. I imagine their training under the *mestres* made them dignified and disciplined musicians, not necessarily entertainers. A few among them stepped out and became brass band leaders (such as Lawry and Chic Chocolate in the film). Donna comes from this background with a pious and anxious mother always keeping her in check.

Matriculation, followed by shorthand and typing, is what many girls did at that time to get into private companies as secretaries and telephone operators. But a spirited Donna cannot be contained. She has her way and joins the band, a not-so-dignified career in those times. For a young and carefree Donna, the line between her and the upper-crust audience doesn't exist. She made the stage her own and mingled with the audience against the wishes of her mentor Lawry.

The three men are the 'three loafers', with Romeo (the conventional village hero) being the leader of the pack. They gather at the local meeting point and exchange the juiciest gossip from the recently arrived seaman who came home after a brief pit stop at the *kudds* in Bombay. The *kudd* residents, too, were all men. So pretty much, it was the men who spread these canards with a little bit of spice.

I used the three loafers as a device, they were the voice of the people, to say things that are difficult to digest. The audience consumes this gossip yet doesn't take the loafers seriously.

RBF: Like a refrain, the theme of drunkenness appears recurrently in your film. The band sings the song 'Bebdo' [Drunkard], which continues to be popular in Goa today and, also, Santan, the washed-up alcoholic played by Prince Jacob, continually reappears at various junctures as comic relief and as the drunken voice of conscience.

Clearly drawing from Bollywood's consistent portrayal of Goans as drunkards, *Nachom-ia Kumpasar* plays against the grain in creating a Goan drunk who has self-awareness of why he is an alcoholic and who sees alcoholism as a symptom of other bigger issues. Santan communicates as much to Donna who slowly descends into alcoholism as the film progresses. Her

FIG. 4. Pisso Santan (Prince Jacob) holds court in
Nachom-ia Kumpasar (2014) by Bardroy Barretto

increasing desire to drown her sorrow in drink is in tandem with the failure of
her romantic relationship and the diminishing fortunes of Goan musicians as
they are sidelined by Bollywood over time. A touchy subject, especially given
how Goans and Goan culture are represented by Indian cinema, why was it
important for you to use drunkenness as a metaphor?

BB: Alcohol is not portrayed as a taboo in *Nachom-ia Kumpasar*; everyone has a
drink at the end of a hard day, yet not everyone shown is an alcoholic, unlike the
Bollywood films, which portray all Goans as drunkards and Goan women in
frocks as women of loose character. Alcohol is synonymous with Goan culture,
be it a wedding or funeral. Also, the famous *feni* is a cure for everything, be it a
headache, toothache, high fever, and even a panacea for love gone wrong.

Pisso Santan [Mad Santan] — is he a drunkard, or is he a madman? He is a
jilted lover; alcohol is his solace, and insanity is his escape from reality. He is
a voice of conscience. Everyone hears him, yet no one listens. Always ignored
by Lawry and the band throughout the film, he eventually succeeds in drawing
Donna into a conversation towards the end of the film. Are they alcoholics, or
are they victims of love gone wrong? Is Donna, too, heading toward insanity?
Their track stops there in the film, leaving the audience to interpret and draw
conclusions themselves.

RBF: Returning to the first rehearsal scene, in the background of the set
one notices a few posters. These include images of Billie Holiday and Louis
Armstrong. While the influence of Black American performers of the jazz era,
and even after, is apparent in the history of Bombay's music scene, it seems that
Goans were particularly attuned to this inspiration.

Chic Chocolate, who appears in your film as a character, is actually fashioned
after a real-life person of the same name. The Aldona-born trumpeter António
Xavier Vaz (1916–1967) christened himself Chic Chocolate and famously

Fig. 5. The band rehearses in *Nachom-ia Kumpasar* (2014) by Bardroy Barretto

modelled his performance style after Louis Armstrong;[6] the two met in Bombay during Armstrong's visit in 1964.[7]

Because of Portuguese colonialism, European classical music training was part of Goan life, but at what point did popular Black American music also become significant in the (Goan and diasporic) zeitgeist?

BB: The trained Goan musicians were introduced to jazz by the early African American jazz bands helmed by Leon Abbey, Cricket Smith, and Teddy Weatherford during the 1930s. The Goan musicians at once took an affinity towards this music. With swing music, they could express themselves, breaking into improvised solos. This expression found its way into Indian cinema too.

It was interesting to re-imagine this world. There were clues in the stage names Goan musicians adopted. Cristovam Perreira became Chris Perry, Franklin Fernandes became Frank Fernand, and António Xavier Vaz became Chic Chocolate, to name a few who ditched their Latin names for English ones. Chic styled himself after his hero Louis Armstrong.

Now, for the prized merchandise of jazz posters seen in the film. Did the musicians get them from the affluent patrons at the jazz clubs as a matter of gratitude? Or did their fellow-Goan seamen get them during their trips overseas?

RBF: So those posters are rather evocative as props! The appearance of Chic Chocolate in your film as a fictionalized person who also was a real musician reminds the audience that the performers you portray were part of Bombay's music history. They brought American Jazz and European classical influences with them and created the sound that would become synonymous with Bollywood. Performers like Anthony Gonsalves (1927–2012), who worked with fabled Goan-origin, Indian film playback singer Lata Mangeshkar (1929–2022), even attempted to synthesize Eastern and Western rhythms.[8]

---

6 Fernandes, *Taj Mahal Foxtrot*, p. 111.
7 Ibid., pp. 168–70.
8 Ibid., pp. 118–20.

Yet, as your film notes, Chic Chocolate was not even recognized for his musical contribution to the film *Albela* (1951), a familiar tale true of the legacy created by many Goan musicians. Why were Goans given short shrift in this regard and, apart from your film and the work done by Naresh Fernandes in *Taj Mahal Foxtrot*, are other efforts underway to address this erasure?

BB: It is widely known that mostly the Hindus were the music directors and the Muslims were the lyricists. The Christian Goan composers and arrangers who played an important role were reduced to the small print or not credited. These three communities used to do the *baithaks* [sittings] and created cult melodies for Indian cinema. The likes of Frank Fernand, Sebastian D'souza, Chic Chocolate, and Anthony Gonsalves, to name a few, changed the soundscape of Indian film music. They introduced harmonies, fado bridges, jazz interludes, and Goan folk rhythms during the Golden Era of Indian cinema. Sebastian D'souza helmed the western orchestra for many decades, Anthony Gonsalves contributed by orchestrating the *ragas*, and Chic Chocolate first introduced swing to Indian films in *Albela*. Sadly, these contributions were not celebrated or recognized.

Taj Mahal Foxtrot and *Nachom-ia Kumpasar* put a spotlight on these unsung musicians. *Wind of Fire: The Music & Musicians of Goa* (1997) by Mario Cabral e Sá is a well-researched book on Goan musicians, both western and Hindustani. *Songit, Doulot Goenkaranchi* [*Music, The Wealth of Goans*] (2004) by Bonaventure D'Pietro is another effort that highlights these musicians. The title of Bonaventure D'Pietro's book is actually the name of a song by M. Boyer, who composed it in either the late 1970s or early 1980s. The song names Goan musicians and the person who actually took credit for their work. The song ends by saying that Goans gave their music to the films but were not credited and were only portrayed as drunkards on screen. These lyrics are what Lawry verbalizes towards the film's end in *Nachom-ia Kumpasar*.

Symphony of Passion (2022) by Melvyn Savio Misquita is one more piece in the jigsaw puzzle which gives Goan musicians the recognition they rightly deserve.

All these glorious musicians deserve at least a Wall of Fame, if not a Hall of Fame. I hope that more and more efforts are put into shining a light on these musicians.

RBF: In closing, what do you see in the future of Goan cinema? What would you like to have it do and what might audiences expect from you next?

BB: The future of Goan cinema is in good hands as many more films are being produced. Out of quantity, we will get quality.

As for me, I will continue to document the Goa of the past in cinema. A film centred around football as a religion set between 1975 and 1985 will be my next film, fingers crossed.

Reviews

RACHEL RANDALL, *Paid to Care: Domestic Workers in Contemporary Latin American Culture* (Austin: University of Texas Press, 2024). x, 288 pages. Print and ebook. doi:10.7560/327708

Reviewed by MEG WEEKS, Assistant Professor, Center for Latin American Studies, University of Florida

Are attitudes toward remunerated domestic work changing in Latin America? One of the region's most enduring phenomena, spanning the colonial and modern eras with remarkably similar patterns of informality and social stratification, paid domestic labour sustains Latin American households yet is typically hidden from public view, tucked away in kitchens and laundry rooms — off the books, under the table. Recent decades, however, have witnessed gains in labour protections for domestic workers from Mexico to Brazil, suggesting a societal reckoning with the practice of employing people to cook, clean, and care for children in private homes. In *Paid to Care: Domestic Workers in Contemporary Latin American Culture*, Rachel Randall makes the case that recent representations of domestic work and domestic workers in film, testimonial literature, digital activism, and public art indicate a growing interest in grappling with the more troubling aspects of the institution. In her introduction, Randall convincingly argues that legislation alone cannot fundamentally alter the subordinated status of the region's domestic workers; as with any social practice, attitudes, moral stances, and appraisals of value must shift to generate the will to pass, enforce, and abide by any particular law. According to Randall, it is in the realm of hearts and minds that art and culture have unique power to intervene: because they are widely distributed and consumed — beloved, despised, or at the very least thought-provoking — cultural representations have the capacity to 'reproduce and rewrite the complex and contradictory foundational narratives' of a nation, to 'denaturalize racialized, gendered, and classed assumptions about who should be doing domestic work and about how paid domestic workers can be treated' (pp. 10, 20).

Throughout the book, Randall uses the terms 'spectral' and 'ghostly' to describe the presence of domestic workers in popular culture: phantom, white-clad figures in the background of candid family photographs, one-dimensional characters in the plots of classic novels, stereotyped comic relief in the cast of a telenovela. Deploying this image of semi-visibility, Randall argues that maids, nannies, and cleaners reside uneasily at the margins of the bourgeois family yet are central to its functioning. On a macro level, she contends, domestic work occupies a similarly fraught position between periphery and core: the practice 'haunts the capitalist economic modes that have never properly accounted for it' (p. 3). In *Paid to Care*, she attempts to remedy this marginalization, placing domestic workers centre stage not only to remind readers of their centrality in Latin American social reproduction, but also to point out the ways in which cultural products can produce radical new epistemologies.

Across four lengthy, rigorously cited chapters, Randall's central concern is the interpersonal (and to a lesser extent legal) mechanisms by which domestic workers are exploited, identifying the ways in which the works she analyses denounce, disrupt, or in some cases shore up, these mechanisms. She is in good company — with scholars of domestic work and socialist feminists alike — in decrying the devaluation of care work and its relegation to the forsaken domain of unproductive labour, devoid of the surplus value typically regarded as the totem of the working class. Building on the scholarship of Encarnación Gutiérrez-Rodríguez and others, Randall argues that not only do domestic workers indeed produce surplus value by reproducing the workforce, sending remittances home to struggling economies, and allowing female employers to pursue a broader range of professional opportunities, they also produce affective value, defined as the positive affects associated with cleanliness, comforting food, well cared for children, and domestic order. Differently from other modes of discursive expression, Randall contends, cultural products possess a singular capacity to capture this affective dimension of paid domestic work, which is precisely the quality that makes the profession so susceptible to abuse. Invoking Clarice Lispector's experimental novel *The Passion According to G.H.* as a point of departure, she frames the classic text as a broader allegory for the Latin American bourgeoisie's feelings of disgust, guilt, and affective ambivalence toward their domestic workers.

In her first chapter, Randall examines several works of testimonial literature, both memoirs and edited collections of first-hand accounts produced with varying degrees of external mediation. In discussing mediation — the ghostwriters, journalists, editors, and scholars who recorded and published the life stories of women of a lower social station — Randall cannot help but engage with Spivak's timeless polemic, 'can the subaltern speak?' Her response to this query, in line with Spivak's own conclusion, is less than sanguine. Yet she is more hopeful for the possibility of subaltern agency in publications that deploy life stories for a collective purpose, those that advocate for the rights of a particular group through social movements and unions. Such is the case with *Se necesita muchacha*, a 1983 compendium of domestic-worker testimonies from Peru, and 'Só a gente que vive é que sabe: depoimento de uma doméstica,' by Lenira Carvalho, one of the most prominent figures in Brazil's domestic-worker movement. Carvalho, whom Randall calls a 'counterhegemonic organic intellectual', uses the form of the *testimonio* — like Rigoberta Menchú, a juggernaut of the genre — as a call to arms, an explication of the ways in which domestic workers are psychologically and physically abused as well as an endorsement of resistance through collective action. Randall distinguishes these two works from *testimonios* that produce essentially individualist narratives of personal hardship and redemption, such as *La niña, el chocolate, el huevo duro* by Ramona Caraballo, and Francisca Souza da Silva's *Ai de vós: diário de uma doméstica*. These stories tend to refrain from structural critiques and are more likely to reinforce, rather than repudiate, the paternalism of the employer–employee relationship: in fact, da Silva's boss authored a preface to her book in which she admits to editing the manuscript to omit passages she determined not to have 'great importance' (p. 46).

Randall takes up this theme of mediation again in her chapter on documentary film. While traditional documentaries tend to feature a single narrator with an authoritative voice, she tells us, more experimental forms disorient the notion of authorship by employing a 'polyphony of voices' (p. 151). Experimental domestic ethnographies such as João Moreira Salles's *Santiago* and Consuelo Lins's *Babás*, critically interrogate the position of the filmmaker vis-à-vis their subjects; in these two films, this reckoning is explicitly incorporated into the narrative, the filmmakers themselves becoming characters in the domestic mise-en-scène. In recent years, both documentaries and fictionalized films have offered their creators opportunities to 'address an emotional obligation' to the domestic workers who raised them, what Mexican director Alfonso Cuarón has called 'a historical debt' (p. 97). In paying tribute to the longsuffering women who laboured in isolation for decades, bereft of legal recourse or the solidarity of union membership, these filmmakers may have commendable motives, but their films, Randall contends, often romanticize the archetypal *mujer abnegada* and 'risk reinforcing foundational myths according to which the forging of the modern mestizo nation-state relies on the subjugation of the racial and gender Other' (p. 88).

Nonetheless, critical darlings like Anna Muylaert's *Que horas ela volta?* and Cuarón's *Roma* can be partially credited with prompting overdue national discussions about the region's centuries-old reliance on the labour of underpaid and mistreated women — often migrants, often Black or indigenous. And their success, Randall seems to suggest, may be due in part to their artistry. In her two chapters on film, Randall deserves credit for her fine-grained analysis of the more subtle aspects of filmmaking. It is not just the plots of these films that are effective as vectors of critique; she argues that filmic techniques themselves are particularly well suited to portraying one of the most blatant symbols of the subordination inherent to paid domestic work: the spatial segregation of private homes. Through her thick and vivid descriptions, we can imagine the 'cinematic trope of the maid's room', the claustrophobia and vexed cohabitation that only an artful camera angle can capture.

For me, the final chapter on digital activism and art (the clunky neologism 'artivism' unfortunately makes an appearance here) was the least theoretically rich of the four. It offered, however, some interesting reflections on the politics of social media influencing, an ambiguous phenomenon that can be a powerful tool for social justice while decidedly not impervious to the commodification and depoliticizing effects of the 'social media attention economy' (p. 201). Randall's succinct conclusion, while serviceable, lacked a discussion of the broader implications of her research, its rather prosaic and abrupt ending foreclosing the possibility of a loftier, more fervent final note on the ethical stakes of her project.

While much recent scholarship has explored the affective entanglements of cleaning, caregiving, bodywork, sex work, and food preparation, Randall's book is novel in exploring how this 'emotional paradox' is presented in works of art and popular culture, which, while they can deliver compelling political commentary, are not always straightforward vehicles of critique in the manner of conventional political discourse (p. 3). That, perhaps, is what renders art more rewarding and fruitful to analyse: its nuance, its ambiguity, its space for unresolved ideas, the artist's freedom to abstain from offering up packaged narratives. While Randall is certainly attentive to these nuances, I found myself puzzled by her use of the term 'ambivalent' as a means of criticizing the cultural products she so carefully analyses. I share the author's ethical commitments to domestic worker resistance, yet I question the impulse to instrumentalize works of art, to reduce them to containers for political messages, the content of which should be unproblematic and beyond reproach. While filmmakers such as Cuarón and Sebastián Silva, who directed 2009's *La nana*, were clearly motivated by a desire to point out the egregious exploitation of domestic workers, they were also undoubtedly compelled to represent the genuine love and care they felt for their nannies, who likely reciprocated this sentiment. The truth of the matter is that there often *is* affective ambivalence in domestic work; situations that are emotionally rewarding in one sense can also be manipulative and harmful in others. Works of art, in their refusal to be tethered to tidy political agendas, are free to explore these ambiguities, even the more troubling ones. Nonetheless, while care work may involve care, it is above all else work. Domestic worker activists will be first to say that even though there may be room for love and affection in one's job, this is no substitute for comprehensive labour protections and benefits. After all, as anti-work theorist Sarah Jaffe reminds us, you can love work, but 'work won't love you back'.[1]

doi:10.1353/port.00018

---

[1]   Sarah Jaffe, *Work Won't Love You Back: How Devotion to Our Jobs Keeps Us Exploited, Exhausted, and Alone* (New York: Bold Type Books, 2021).

PAULO DE MEDEIROS and JOSÉ N. ORNELAS (eds), *Saramago After the Nobel: Contemporary Readings of José Saramago's Late Works* (Oxford: Peter Lang, 2022). viii, 280 pages. Print and ebook. doi:10.3726/b11614

Reviewed by MARGARIDA RENDEIRO (CHAM, NOVA FCSH, Lisbon)

Saramago After the Nobel: Contemporary Readings of José Saramago's Late Works (henceforth *Saramago After the Nobel*) is an edited volume featuring essays, written in English, by fourteen scholars, many of whom have established reputations through peer-reviewed publications. These scholars have made significant contributions to the critical discourse on the work of Portuguese author José Saramago, particularly on those published before the Nobel Prize. Notable among their previous works are Adriana Alves de Paula Martins's *A Construção da Memória da Nação em José Saramago e Gore Vidal* (2006);[2] David Frier's *The Novels of José Saramago: Echoes from the Past, Pathways into the Future* (2007);[3] and Paulo de Medeiros and José Ornelas's *Da Possibilidade do Impossível: Leituras de Saramago* (2007), an edited volume resulting from the first international conference on Saramago's work, held in 1996 at the University of Massachusetts Amherst with the author's attendance.[4] More recently, Mark Sabine's *José Saramago: History, Utopia, and the Necessity of Error* (2016) further adds to this body of scholarship.[5]

Paulo de Medeiros and José Ornelas, once again collaborating as editors, highlight Saramago's 'transformative force, both as a writer and as a public intellectual' (p. 1). This volume is a timely and valuable contribution to the study of Saramago's works, published in the year marking the Portuguese author's centenary. *Saramago After the Nobel* addresses a critical gap in the literature on his post-Nobel works, as noted in the Introduction, where the editors argue that there has been a 'deficit, whether real or perceived' in the attention given to these later writings (p. 2). By thoroughly analysing these works within the context of Saramago's broader literary career, the volume significantly enhances our understanding of his *oeuvre*. The Introduction stresses that excluding Saramago's post-Nobel works from critical discussions would result in 'unnatural' and 'misguided' interpretations, creating an 'artificial barrier where none exists' (p. 2). The editors thus advocate for a re-examination of his later works through a twenty-first-century lens, emphasizing their relevance to contemporary debates and global issues. Saramago's writings continue to resonate with modern concerns and this volume illustrates how his works remain profoundly relevant today. The global attention Saramago's works

[2] Adriana Alves de Paula Martins, *A Construção da Memória da Nação em José Saramago e Gore Vidal* (Frankfurt: Peter Lang, 2006).
[3] David Frier, *The Novels of José Saramago: Echoes from the Past, Pathways into the Future* (Cardiff: University of Wales Press, 2007).
[4] Paulo de Medeiros and José Ornelas (eds), *Da Possibilidade do Impossível: Leituras de Saramago* (Utrecht: Universiteit Utrecht, 2007).
[5] Mark Sabine, *José Saramago: History, Utopia, and the Necessity of Error* (Cambridge: Legenda, 2016).

attract is evident in the contributors' affiliations with institutions in various countries, including the United States, the United Kingdom, Portugal, and the United Arab Emirates, demonstrating the enduring academic interest in his literary legacy.

José Saramago was not only a talented and multifaceted writer but also a figure deeply engaged with global issues, using his platform to address them. Three essays in this volume explore the extent to which he embodied this global identity. In the opening essay, Mark Sabine argues compellingly that after receiving his Nobel Prize in 1998, Saramago skilfully leveraged his cultural capital to maintain control over his public image and the influence of his literary work until his death in 2010. In the following essay, Paulo de Medeiros asserts that Saramago's position as a semi-peripheral writer, in the context of world-systems theory, gave him a heightened awareness of global inequalities, which he poignantly reflected in his works. This perspective, Medeiros argues, makes Saramago deeply contemporary in the sense discussed by Giorgio Agamben. Carlos Nogueira, in his essay, focuses on *The Cave* and also examines Saramago's early short story 'Os animais loucos de cólera' from *Deste Mundo e do Outro* (1960s), and the 2008 manifesto *Novo Capitalismo?* that Saramago endorsed. Nogueira highlights Saramago's enduring, ethical and moral stance on ecology and the politics of nature, which is consistently reflected in his works. Throughout his career, Saramago advocated for a more harmonious way of inhabiting the Earth, a theme that permeates both his literary creations and public engagements.

Several essays in this volume reveal unexpected connections between Saramago's works and those of other authors, offering fresh perspectives on his literary contributions. One notable example is Hania A. M. Nashef's essay, which examines *Death at Intervals* within the framework of World Literature. Drawing on Heidegger's concept of *Da-sein*, Hania explores parallels between Saramago's novel and Palestinian poet Mahmoud Darwish's long poem *Mural*, arguing that both works depict the moment of dying as the realization of the 'absolute impossibility' of *Da-sein* — the point at which one fully embraces humanity and reaches one's potential as a person. In another essay, Aline Ferreira discusses *The Double*, extending the analysis to include Henry James's *The Sense of the Past* and Daphne du Maurier's *The Scapegoat*. Ferreira identifies similarities in how these works address their protagonists' encounters with their doubles, arguing that Saramago's novel can be read as a parable about the fear of standardization in contemporary society and as a cautionary tale on the unethical use of reproductive technologies.

The significance of dogs in Saramago's works has been a subject of previous academic study, notably in Carlo Salzani's essay from the volume he co-edited with Kristof Vanhoutte (2018) on Saramago's philosophical heritage.[6] While

---

[6]   Carlo Salzani, 'Saramago's Dogs: For an Inclusive Humanism', in *José Saramago's Philosophical Heritage*, ed. by Carlo Salzani and Kristof Vanhoutte (Cham: Palgrave Macmillan, 2018), pp. 193–210.

Salzani focused on the symbolic role of dogs in philosophical contexts, Estela Vieira's essay in *Saramago After the Nobel* expands the discussion by exploring the symbolic importance of the dog in *Blindness*, Saramago's last novel published before his Nobel Prize. Vieira offers a comparative analysis of the dog's symbolism in Mozambican Luís Bernardo Honwana's 'We Killed Mangy Dog' and Francisco de Goya's painting *The Drowning Dog.* She argues that dogs, as alienated yet human-like figures, serve as metaphors for shared humanity, empathy, and pathos. This essay illustrates how rereading Saramago's works through the lens of World Literature opens new avenues for exploring these themes.

Every work Saramago published between 1998 and 2010 is discussed in this volume, with most receiving critical exploration in multiple essays. Notable exceptions include *The Elephant's Journey,* which is examined only in Adriana Alves de Paula Martins's essay, and *As Pequenas Memórias* (2006), analysed by Orlando Grossegesse alongside *Handbook of Painting and Calligraphy* and *Death at Intervals.* The various essays — typically two on each of Saramago's other works — offer complementary perspectives that enrich our understanding of his literary output. A notable example is the treatment of *Cain,* discussed in essays by José Ornelas and Manuel Frias Martins. Both contributors examine *Cain* with *The Gospel According to Jesus Christ* in mind, analysing Saramago's engagement with the Bible to deconstruct the Holy Scriptures as records of a profound misunderstanding between the concept of God, as portrayed in the Bible, and humanity. Ornelas argues that Saramago's parody of Cain reflects historical, ideological, and ethical differences, distancing itself from the foundational myths and symbols, and official history of the Bible. Frias Martins offers a balanced comparison of the two novels, contending that Saramago's humanization of Christ and Cain serves to restore the compassion and kindness absent in the religious texts and institutions that traditionally depict these figures without human empathy.

Saramago After the Nobel also explores Saramago's plays, particularly *Don Giovanni ou o Dissoluto Absolvido.* Both David Frier and Sara Lima e Sousa examine this work, though from distinct perspectives. Lima e Sousa focuses on the use of parody in the play, as developed by Azio Corghi and Saramago in the text, libretto, and stage performance. She argues that the use of mannequins as stand-ins for dead bodies during the opera mediates and softens the depiction of death in a way that written text alone cannot achieve. Frier, on the other hand, examines the voices of women in the play, drawing on Foucault's *Discipline and Punish* to address the problematic gender dynamics in *Don Giovanni.*[7] Revisiting the portrayal of women in Saramago's earlier works, as analysed by Ana Paula Ferreira (2001),[8] Frier argues persuasively that Saramago's use of

---

[7] Michel Foucault, *Discipline and Punish: The Birth of the Prison,* trans. by Alan Sheridan, 2nd edn (London: Vintage Press, 1995).
[8] Ana Paula Ferreira, 'Cruising Gender in the Eighties (from *Levantado do Chão* to *The History of the*

historical revisionism risks perpetuating gender oppression by denying women full agency, often rendering them passive in relation to male protagonists.

As noted earlier, *Saramago After the Nobel* was published in the centenary year of Saramago and is a significant contribution to the study of his work. While this thought-provoking volume primarily focuses on his post-Nobel writings, it also sheds light on his broader literary career, underscoring the lasting relevance and contemporaneity of his work.

doi:10.1353/port.00019

CONCEIÇÃO LIMA, *No Gods Live Here: Selected Poems*, translated by Shook (Dallas, TX: Phoneme Media; Deep Vellum, 2024). 255 pages. Print and ebook.

Reviewed by ROBERT PATRICK NEWCOMB (University of California, Davis)

No Gods Live Here presents a career-spanning, bilingual selection of work by the Santomean poet Conceição Lima (b. 1961), in which the original Portuguese texts are presented alongside English translations. Lima published the first of her four poetry collections, *O Útero da Casa* [The Womb of the House] in 2004, and has since emerged as a major voice in Santomean letters, following in the tradition of Caetano da Costa Alegre, Francisco José Tenreiro, and Alda do Espírito Santo. She is also a key figure in the broader field of contemporary Lusophone poetry and should be considered a major contemporary African poet; hopefully the publication of *No Gods Live Here*, which makes so much of her work available in English translation, will raise her profile beyond the Portuguese-speaking world.

Among her many merits as a poet, Lima is notable for her sophisticated examination of how cultures and individuals are formed through the interplay of dialectically opposed forces such as rootedness and exile, presence and absence, and generosity and cruelty. Lima's observations are broadly applicable: what person or group is *not* the product of contradiction? However, they are also grounded in her homeland's specific history. São Tomé and Príncipe, is, as Lima puts it, an 'Afroinsular' country comprised of two islands and several islets located just north of the equator, off Africa's Atlantic coast. It is the smallest of the five countries that prior to 1974–75 constituted Portugal's African colonies. When the Portuguese first arrived in the late fifteenth century, the islands were uninhabited. São Tomé and Príncipe's population is descended overwhelmingly from enslaved and, later, coerced Africans whom the Portuguese brought from the continent and from Cabo Verde over the centuries to work in brutal conditions on sugar and, later, cacao plantations. The islands' history of displacement, exploitation, and disenfranchisement, but also of ethnogenesis, cultural formation, and nation-building, leads Lima to ponder several difficult questions for herself and her fellow Santomeans: How can one be 'rooted' in an island when one is also 'displaced', in an ancestral sense, from continental Africa? Can islands that have been places of exile also be 'home'? And finally, how can a culture be built from unimaginable suffering, that is, 'quando impassível marchou a infernal engrenagem | e o mundo emergiu' [when the infernal gear shifted impassively | and the world emerged], as she writes in 'Espanto' [Astonishment] (pp. 72–73)?

Lima employs several techniques to draw out these complexities. First, she often describes contradiction through oxymoron, as in her reference to 'ambíguas claridades' [ambiguous clarities] in 'Afroinsularidade' [Afroinsularity], as well as paradox, as when she states of an enslaved African in colonial São Tomé, 'terá sofrido no Equador o frio da Gronelândia' [even here, on the equator, he would have ached with the chill of Greenland] in the stunning 'Canto Obscuro às Raízes' [Dark Song to My Roots]. She also makes several references to transmutation, as in 'Espanto,' in which she describes the history of her islands as follows: 'A Ocidente se abriu uma vanguarda de tumbas | que expande do deserto a metamorfose | em novos hinos, outros abismos chamados ilhas [The West unfurled a frontline of tombs | that expands metamorphosis from the desert | in new hymns, other abysses called islands] (pp. 38–39, 58–59, 72–73). Second, she frequently employs the terms *raiz* and *raízes* [root, roots], and often opposes images and ideas of rootedness to uprooting, displacement, or death. In 'Roça' [Plantation] the poetic voice asks: 'Perguntam os mortos: || Porque brotam raízes dos nossos pés? || [...] Que reino foi esse que plantámos?' [The dead ask: || Why do roots sprout from our feet? || [...] What was this kingdom that we planted?] (pp. 32–33). Elsewhere she refers to 'outras cargas sem sonhos nem raízes' [other dreamless, rootless cargos] in 'Afroinsularidade' (pp. 36–37), and to 'esta raiz enxertada de epitáfios' [this root grafted with epitaphs] in 'A Mão' [The Hand] (pp. 82–83). Finally, Lima routinely invokes absent or displaced gods, referring to their absence *from* São Tomé and Príncipe, as when she declares in 'Arquipélago' [Archipelago] that 'aqui não moram deuses' [no gods live here] (pp. 84–85), and to the idea that African gods — and perhaps African cultures and cosmovisions generally — are exiled in the islands, as when she refers to '[a] indelével lembrança dos deuses | Desterrados' [the indelible memory of gods | In exile] in 'Em Santana' [In Santana] (pp. 42–43). Lima often seems reluctant to resolve these admittedly productive contradictions, though she occasionally presents language and poetry as somehow transcending the violent oppositions of worldly life, and as privileged vehicles for clear expression, as in her recent prose poem 'A Lição dos Pássaros' [The Birds' Lesson], which concludes as follows: 'Qualquer ambiguidade é um sóbrio chamamento: não há desterro para a palavra' [Any ambiguity is a sober summons: there is no banishment for the word] (pp. 236–37).

I find Shook's English translations, which they undertook in collaboration with Lima, to be skilful and assured. In terms of style, Shook is particularly successful in conveying Lima's frequent use of alliteration and assonance even when Portuguese and English provide different opportunities for these, as in 'Mostra-me o Sangue da Lua' [Show Me the Moon's Blood]. Here Lima refers to 'a náusea do mar | e o nojo das rochas,' which Shook translates as 'the sea's nausea | and the rocks' revulsion' (pp. 30–31; my emphasis). In terms of accuracy, having read most of these poems in the original prior to picking up *No Gods Live Here*, I find myself largely in agreement with Shook's choices. For instance, in Lima's 'Arquipélago', they render the declaration 'aqui não moram deuses' as 'no gods live here.' While 'gods don't live here' would also be accurate, it is more prosaic and lacks the punch of 'no gods live here', which, besides, provides Lima and Shook with a memorable title for the collection. Shook's translations are populated with smart choices like these.

In sum, I wholeheartedly recommend *No Gods Live Here*. This collection will certainly be of interest to readers of Conceição Lima, to specialists in and students of Lusophone and African poetry — not to mention Lusophone African poetry — and to anyone interested in spending some time with an extraordinary contemporary poet.

doi:10.1353/port.00020

Abstracts

Palimpsestic Orientalism: Deciphering the Layered Reconstructions of the Portuguese-Macau Film Co-production *The Bewitching Braid* (1996)
YUXUAN LIU

ABSTRACT. The present study examines the epistemological underpinnings of Orientalism, as embedded in the collective psyche of the Macanese community, through the lens of Henrique de Senna Fernandes's celebrated novel *A trança feiticeira* [*The Bewitching Braid*] and the 1996 film adaptation of the same name, directed by Yuanyuan Cai. It focuses on the intersection of colonial narratives and Orientalist thought, uncovering the psychological divide that has long rationalized systemic exploitation and dominance over the Other through a blend of literary criticism and film analysis. The novel and its cinematic representation, which delve deep into native Macanese identity across historical epochs, have not been examined from an Orientalist perspective. The present study fills this gap by dissecting the intricate layers of Orientalism and narrative development in Fernandes's work, offering new insights into the construction of Macanese identity and associated cultural narratives. The profound social fissures, racial complexities, and power imbalances concealed within the film's layers are uncovered, and the timeless themes of identity, cultural integration, and social tensions that have permeated Macau's history and Sino-Portuguese relations and shaped the region are discussed in detail.

KEYWORDS. Orientalism; Macanese identity; Henrique de Senna Fernandes; *The Bewitching Braid*; Yuanyuan Cai; Sino-Portuguese relations; Macau; fiction film; interracial relationships.

RESUMO. Este artigo examina como os fundamentos epistemológicos do orientalismo, tal como se encontram incorporados na psique coletiva da comunidade macaense, se revelam no célebre romance de Henrique de Senna Fernandes, *A trança feiticeira*, e na adaptação cinematográfica homónima de 1996, realizada por Yuanyuan Cai. O livro centra-se na intersecção das narrativas coloniais e do pensamento orientalista, revelando a divisão psicológica que há muito racionaliza a exploração sistémica e o domínio sobre o Outro, através de uma mistura de crítica literária e análise cinematográfica. O romance e a sua representação cinematográfica, que se aprofundam na identidade nativa macaense ao longo de épocas históricas, não foram examinados de uma perspetiva orientalista. O presente estudo preenche esta lacuna ao dissecar as intrincadas camadas de orientalismo e desenvolvimento narrativo na obra de Fernandes, oferecendo novas perspetivas sobre a construção da identidade

Portuguese Studies vol. 40 no. 2 (2024), doi:10.1353/port.00021, pp. 239–46
© Modern Humanities Research Association 2024

macaense e as narrativas culturais associadas. São reveladas as profundas fissuras sociais, complexidades raciais e desequilíbrios de poder ocultos nas camadas do filme, e são discutidos em pormenor os temas intemporais da identidade, da integração cultural e das tensões sociais que têm permeado a história de Macau e as relações sino-portuguesas e que moldaram a região.

PALAVRAS-CHAVE. Orientalismo; identidade macaense; Henrique de Senna Fernandes; *A trança feiticeira*; Yuanyuan Cai; relações sino-portuguesas; Macau; filme de ficção, relações interraciais.

'Portuguese India': Between the Desire for a Konkani Cinema and the Paradoxes of Filmed Propaganda
MARIA DO CARMO PIÇARRA

ABSTRACT. The range of Portuguese films focusing on the 'Orient' during the *Estado Novo* is scant, late, and persistently inclined to affirming a Luso-tropicalist rhetoric that contributes to the renewing of the myth around the (lost) importance of a territory which, during the dictatorship, retained little more than symbolic importance. In this article, I focus on 'Portuguese India', where, notwithstanding a vibrant film exhibition culture, Konkani cinema never gained traction, but where we can still recognize a simultaneous stream of propaganda films that aimed to project the image of a supposed Luso-tropical idyll, favouring religious themes, and extoling multiculturalism and miscegenation — concomitantly contradicted by the tensions manifest in films with a political-military focus. I propose that the lack of Portuguese films resulted not just from a physical distance from the metropolis and the costs of production. Despite the regime's tardiness in stimulating and supporting the filming of these territories, the symbolic value of that 'imagined community' was better disseminated by a kind of cinematic omission. When production did take place, it ignored certain aspects of reality as much as it filmed others, framing them inside a vague Luso-oriental rhetoric which concealed anything that contradicted the prevalent 'order of discourse'.

KEYWORDS. Luso-tropicalism; 'Portuguese India'; Konkani cinema; 'imagined community'; Orient; Estado Novo; propaganda films; dictatorship; colonial cinema.

RESUMO. A produção de filmes portugueses sobre o 'Oriente' durante o Estado Novo foi escassa, tardia e persistiu, genericamente, na afirmação de uma retórica luso-tropicalista contributiva para a renovação do mito em torno da importância (perdida) de um território que, durante a ditadura, pouco mais teve do que importância simbólica. Neste artigo, concentro-me na 'Índia Portuguesa', onde, apesar de uma vibrante cultura de exibição cinematográfica, o cinema em língua concanim nunca ganhou força, num contexto em que, simultaneamente, é detetável um fluxo pontual de filmes de propaganda, tanto em termos de produção como de exibição, com que o regime português visou projetar um imaginário caracterizado pelo suposto idílio luso-tropical, privilegiando temas religiosos e exaltando o multiculturalismo e a miscigenação — concomitantemente contraditados pelas tensões manifestadas em filmes com um enfoque político-militar. Proponho que a raridade de filmes portugueses relativos à 'Índia Portuguesa' não resultou apenas da distância física da metrópole e dos custos de produção. Apesar da demora do regime em estimular e apoiar a filmagem destes territórios, o valor simbólico dessa 'comunidade imaginada' foi imposto mais facilmente através de uma espécie de omissão cinematográfica. Quando o fluxo de produção propagandística sucedeu, tanto ignorou certos aspetos da realidade como filmou outros enquadrando-os através de uma vaga retórica luso-oriental que ocultava tudo o que contrariasse a 'ordem do discurso' vigente.

PALAVRAS-CHAVE. Luso-tropicalismo; 'Índia Portuguesa'; cinema concanim; 'comunidade imaginada'; Oriente; Estado Novo; filmes de propaganda; ditadura; cinema colonial.

A Transcivilizational Island: Paulo Rocha's *A Ilha dos Amores*

PAULO CUNHA

ABSTRACT. Directed by the Portuguese Paulo Rocha and premiered at the Cannes Film Festival in 1982, *A Ilha dos Amores* [The Island of Love] is a film about the relationship between West and East as seen through the eyes of the Portuguese poet and diplomat Wenceslau de Moraes. Born in Lisbon in 1854, Moraes lived in Macau from 1891 until 1898 and between 1898 and 1913 he was stationed in Japan, where he would die in 1929. Rocha's film is also marked by the work of two poets: the Chinese poet Chu Yuan (343 BC–278 BC) and the Portuguese poet Luís Vaz de Camões (1524–1580). The intersection of these varied literary and cultural universes turns this cinematic narrative into a transcivilizational object. The aim of this essay is to understand these relationships and to reflect upon the mediating role of cinema as a powerful instrument for evoking and reframing the past.

KEYWORDS. Cinema; transnational; literature; theatre, Orient.

RESUMO. Estreado no Festival de Cannes, em 1982, realizado pelo português Paulo Rocha, *A Ilha dos Amores* é um filme que fala da relação entre o Ocidente e o Oriente a partir da vida do poeta e diplomata português Wenceslau de Moraes, que nasceu em Lisboa (1854), e viveu em Macau (1891–98) e no Japão (1898–1929), onde morreu. O filme é também marcado pela obra do poeta chinês Chu Yuan (343 a.C.–278 a.C.) e do poeta português Luís Vaz de Camões (1524–1580), num cruzamento de universos literários e culturais que torna esta narrativa transcivilizacional. O objetivo deste texto é compreender estas relações e refletir sobre o papel mediador do cinema na evocação e ressignificação do passado.

PALAVRAS-CHAVE. Cinema; transnacional; literatura; teatro; Oriente.

Entre eu e Deus by Yara Costa: An Unprecedented Representation of the Island of Mozambique
JESSICA FALCONI

ABSTRACT. Set on the Island of Mozambique, *Entre eu e Deus* [Between God and I] (2018) is the third film by Mozambican director Yara Costa and brings an original representation of a crucial place in the Mozambican cultural imagination. During the period of colonial domination, but more especially after independence, the cultural representation of the Island of Mozambique has been confronted with a fundamental aspect, constitutive of the imaginary relating to this place: its role as an entrepôt for commercial, cultural and religious routes before and after the arrival of the Portuguese. This role contributed to the emergence of distinct and sometimes opposing representations of the Island, which were later appropriated and recreated by different discourses.

After a brief historical and cultural contextualization of the Island of Mozambique, this article analyses the documentary by Yara Costa with the primary objective of demonstrating that it sets out to challenge images, representations and crystallized perceptions about the Island of Mozambique, Mozambican cultural identity and Islamic fundamentalism, and that it succeeds in doing so.

KEYWORDS. Island of Mozambique; Mozambican cultural identity; Islamic fundamentalism; Yara Costa.

RESUMO. Ambientado na Ilha de Moçambique, *Entre eu e Deus* (2018) é o terceiro filme da realizadora moçambicana Yara Costa e traz uma representação original de um lugar crucial no imaginário cultural moçambicano. Quer durante a dominação colonial, mas sobretudo após a independência, a representação cultural da Ilha de Moçambique tem sido confrontada com um aspeto fundamental, constitutivo do imaginário relativo a este lugar: o seu papel como entreposto de rotas comerciais, culturais e religiosas antes e depois da chegada dos portugueses. Este papel contribuiu para o surgimento de representações distintas e por vezes opostas da Ilha, que foram posteriormente apropriadas e recriadas por diferentes discursos.

Após uma breve contextualização histórica e cultural da Ilha de Moçambique, este artigo analisa o documentário de Yara Costa com o objetivo principal de demonstrar que este pretende, e consegue, desafiar imagens, representações e perceções cristalizadas sobre a Ilha de Moçambique, a identidade cultural moçambicana e o fundamentalismo islâmico.

PALAVRAS-CHAVE. Ilha de Moçambique; identidade cultural moçambicana; fundamentalismo islâmico; Yara Costa.

East Timor in Margarida Gil's *Bitter Flowers*: The Power of the Unrooted Underdog

ANA ISABEL SOARES

ABSTRACT. In this essay, I propose a detailed analysis of Margarida Gil's film *Flores Amargas* [*Bitter Flowers*] (1989) to appreciate the multiplicity of European perspectives — that of the Portuguese colonizer — on a very particular Asia, namely East Timor. Margarida Gil's feature adopts a quasi-fictional tone while the action is set among an East Timorese community in Vale do Jamor, on the outskirts of Lisbon, which it also documents. The Timorese are characterized as a homogeneous and relatively tight-knit group who retain the habits and traditions of their geographically distant homeland while apparently accepting the welcoming linguistic environment it shares with the post-colonial metropolis. Amidst readings of paternalism, zeal for cultural heritage and layers of domination, the film establishes a primarily human geography, based on gazes and facial expressions, in which the work of light and shade plays a fundamental role.

East Timor was revisited in Gil's filmic work nine years later in *Anjo da Guarda* [*Guardian Angel*] (1998); in this work, the Asian territory serves as a backdrop to the memories of a recently deceased father and for the Freudian tribulations of a psychiatrist going through a mid-life crisis. I suggest an allegorical reading of the end of the colonizing homeland and the difficulty of affirming the new Portugal, grappling with the emotional relationship with a past whose memory does not fade.

KEYWORDS. Margarida Gil; East Timor; Portuguese cinema; post-colonial cinema; *Bitter Flowers*; Timorese; colonial gaze.

RESUMO. Neste ensaio, parto de uma análise de pormenor do filme *Flores Amargas* (Margarida Gil, 1989) para entender a multiplicidade de olhares do europeu (o colonizador português) sobre uma Ásia muito particular (Timor-Leste). A obra de Margarida Gil desenrola-se num registo próximo do ficcional, mas ambientado numa comunidade timorense do Vale do Jamor, nos arredores de Lisboa, que igualmente documenta. O grupo de timorenses é caracterizado como homogéneo e relativamente fechado — revive os hábitos e as tradições da pátria geograficamente distante, mas parece aceitar como acolhedor o ambiente linguístico que partilha com a metrópole pós-colonial. Entre leituras de paternalismo, zelo pelo património cultural e camadas de dominação, o filme fixa uma geografia particularmente humana, assente sobre olhares e rostos, em que o trabalho de iluminação e obscurecimento cumpre um papel fundamental.

Timor-Leste regressou à obra de Margarida Gil nove anos depois, quando, em *Anjo da Guarda* (1998), o território asiático serviu de fundo à narrativa das memórias de um pai recentemente falecido e às atribulações freudianas de uma psiquiatra em crise de meia-idade. Sugiro uma leitura alegórica do fim da pátria colonizadora e da dificuldade de afirmação do novo Portugal, a braços com a relação emocional com um passado cuja lembrança não se extingue.

PALAVRAS-CHAVE. Margarida Gil; Timor-Leste; cinema português; cinema pós-colonial; *Flores Amargas*; timorenses; olhar colonial.

Adventures in Mozambique and the Portuguese Tendency to Forget: A Radical Critique of Portuguese Late Colonialism by Ângela Ferreira
LURDES MACEDO and VIVIANE ALMEIDA

ABSTRACT. This article aims to present a critical reflection on the way in which the film *Adventures in Mozambique and the Portuguese Tendency to Forget*, directed by Ângela Ferreira, contrasts two realities experienced in Mozambique during the late colonial period — that of the Portuguese settlers and that of the indigenous Maconde — through an artistic composition departing from a reinterpretation of four archives. The image archives refer to *Mozambique: On the Other Side of Time* and *Margot Dias: Ethnographic Films, 1958–1961*, which Ferreira alternates and combines with sound narratives based on the testimonials of Margot Dias in her diaries and Jorge Dias in his reports, as ethnologists who had studied the Maconde of Mozambique.

The hypothesis put forward to open this reflection is that *Adventures in Mozambique* constitutes a radical critique of the Portuguese colonial system in this territory in the 1950s to 1970s, based on the application of the concept of 'return of the gaze' renewed by Ferreira to her methodology of constructing the filmic object. To essay this hypothesis, we mainly analysed *Adventures in Mozambique* and the original films used to compose it, we revised literature both generally and especially on the key concept of 'the return of the gaze', and we interviewed the artist.

The conclusions point out that by applying her own concept of 'the return of the gaze' to make this film, Ferreira proposes three possibilities: the creative, which is relate with 'the return of the gaze' of the camera; the relational, connected with 'the return of the gaze' of the spectator; and the communicative, that finally allowed the artist to say what she wanted to say about the late colonialism in Mozambique through evidence of the Dias couple's spying activities that went beyond Ethnology.

KEYWORDS. Ângela Ferreira; *A Tendency to Forget*; Portuguese late colonialism; Mozambique; Jorge and Margot Dias.

RESUMO. Este artigo tem como objetivo apresentar uma reflexão crítica sobre o modo como o filme *Adventures in Mozambique and the Portuguese Tendency to Forget*, realizado por Ângela Ferreira, contrasta duas realidades vividas em Moçambique durante o período colonial tardio — a dos colonos portugueses e a dos indígenas macondes — através de uma composição artística que parte da reinterpretação de quatro arquivos. Os arquivos de imagens referem-se a *Moçambique: Do Outro Lado do Tempo* e *Margot Dias: Filmes Etnográficos 1958-1961*, que Ferreira intercala e combina com narrativas sonoras baseadas nos testemunhos de Margot Dias nos seus diários, e de Jorge Dias nos seus relatórios, enquanto etnólogos que estudaram os Maconde de Moçambique.

A hipótese avançada para abrir esta reflexão é a de que *Adventures in Mozambique and the Portuguese Tendency to Forget* constitui uma crítica radical ao sistema colonial português neste território nos anos 1950–1970, a partir da aplicação do conceito 'the return of the gaze', renovado por Ferreira, à sua metodologia de construção do objeto fílmico. Para ensaiar esta hipótese, analisámos sobretudo *Adventures in Mozambique and the Portuguese Tendency to Forget* e os filmes originais que o compõem, fizemos uma revisão de literatura em geral e em particular sobre o conceito-chave 'the return of the gaze', e entrevistámos a artista. As conclusões apontam para o facto de que, ao aplicar o seu próprio conceito 'the return of the gaze' na realização deste filme, Ferreira propõe três possibilidades: a criativa, que se relaciona com o 'the return of the gaze' da câmara; a relacional, ligada ao 'the return of the gaze' do espetador; e a comunicativa, que permitiu à artista dizer finalmente o que queria dizer sobre o colonialismo tardio em Moçambique ao evidenciar as atividades de espionagem do casal Dias para além da Etnologia.

PALAVRAS-CHAVE. Ângela Ferreira; *A Tendency to Forget*; colonialismo tardio português; Moçambique; Jorge e Margot Dias.

How Bollywood Lost its Goan Rhythm: An Interview with Bardroy Barretto, Director of *Nachom-ia Kumpasar*
R. BENEDITO FERRÃO

ABSTRACT. In this interview with Bardroy Barretto, director of the Konkani-language film *Nachom-ia Kumpasar* (2014), we discuss its chronicling of the contribution of Goan musicians to the Golden Era of Indian cinema (late 1940s to 1960s). Set in Goa and Bombay of the 1960s, Barretto's film fictionalizes the period by portraying the lives of musicians who are, in turn, inspired by real-life Goan entertainers, such as Lorna Cordeiro, Chris Perry, and others. Even as the film demonstrates how Goan music with its Portuguese influences created the soundtrack for Bollywood in the second half of the twentieth century, *Nachom-ia Kumpasar* also bears witness to the part played by the Indian film industry and film history in undermining the legacy of Goan musicians. Additionally, the interview includes Barretto's perspective on how Bombay became a site of possibility for Goans at the end of Portuguese colonialism, their forays into entertainment giving rise to Goan, Konkani-language theatre (*tiatr*) and film, as well. Further, as *Nachom-ia Kumpasar* and its director evidence, Goan musicians not only brought their Portuguese colonial-era musical training to Bollywood, but also the rhythms of jazz. While such musical histories may be forgotten, and as Barretto's film and this interview make clear, the mark Goans left on Indian cinema's soundscape cannot fail to be heard.

KEYWORDS. Goa; Bollywood; *Tiatr* (theatre); Jazz; Portuguese India.

RESUMO. Na entrevista com Bardroy Barretto, realizador do filme em língua konkani *Nachom-ia Kumpasar* (2014), discute-se o seu retrato da contribuição dos músicos goeses para a Era de Ouro do cinema indiano (finais dos anos 1940–1960). Passado em Goa e Bombaim na década de 1960, o filme de Barretto ficcionaliza o período retratando a vida de músicos que, por sua vez, são inspirados por artistas goeses da vida real, como Lorna Cordeiro, Chris Perry, e outros. Ao mesmo tempo que demonstra como a música goesa, com as suas influências portuguesas, influenciou fortemente as bandas sonoras da produção de Bollywood na segunda metade do século XX, *Nachom-ia Kumpasar* também testemunha o papel desempenhado pela indústria cinematográfica indiana e pela história do cinema na subestimação do legado dos músicos goeses. Além disso, a entrevista inclui a perspetiva de Barretto sobre a forma como Bombaim se tornou um local de oportunidades para os goeses no final do colonialismo português, e como as experiências destes na indústria do entretenimento originaram o teatro (*tiatr*) e o cinema em língua konkani de Goa. Além disso, como demonstram *Nachom-ia Kumpasar* e o seu realizador, os músicos goeses não só trouxeram para Bollywood a sua formação musical da era colonial portuguesa, como também os ritmos do jazz. Embora essas histórias musicais possam ser esquecidas, e como o filme de Barretto e esta entrevista deixam claro, a marca que os goeses deixaram na paisagem sonora do cinema indiano não pode deixar de ser ouvida.

PALAVRAS-CHAVE. Goa; Bollywood; *Tiatr* (teatro); Jazz; Índia Portuguesa.

9 781839 542855